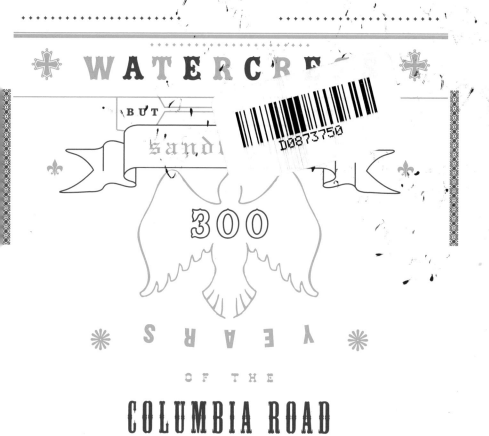

WATERCRE

BUT

sand

300

YEARS

OF THE

COLUMBIA ROAD

A R E A

"When I ask for a watercress sandwich, I do not mean a loaf with a field in the middle of it." OSCAR WILDE

Words: Linda Wilkinson
Design: Barnbrook Studio
Jonathan Barnbrook
Jason Beard
Marcus McCallion
Pedro Sardenberg

New Photography: Tomoko Yoneda

JHERA would like to thank all those residents
who so kindly donated money for this project.

Made possible by Awards for All

*This book was produced using
Adobe InDesign 1.5 and Adobe Photoshop 6.0*

Published by JHERA
ISBN 0-9546840-0-1

This print run was made possible by Tom Mulligan,
director Bridge Estates, as a thank you to the con-
tinuing support from the residents of Jesus Green.
www.bridge-estates.com
020 7749 1400

CONTENTS

INTRO — duction

Until recently
BETHNAL GREEN

HAS BEEN ALMOST EXCLUSIVELY ASSOCIATED WITH POVERTY AND CRIME. DURING THE SECOND WORLD WAR THE IMAGE OF THE IMPOVERISHED INHABITANTS OF LONDON'S HEARTLAND WAS USED TO CREATE THE MYTH OF AN INDOMITABLE POPULATION ABLE TO WITHSTAND EVERYTHING THE LUFTWAFFE COULD THROW AT IT. NOWADAYS THE PROGRAM EAST ENDERS ON TELEVISION IS EXPANDING AND EMBELLISHING THIS MYTH FOR MILLIONS OF VIEWERS AROUND THE WORLD.

Albert Square is of course a confection, a convenience used to build a soap-opera upon the foundations of these myths. Poverty, when generic, breeds its own needs and fairy tales and East London has no exclusive rights upon these. Yet there is something special about East London which the bombings of the wars and the wholesale demolition of the 1960s has not managed to eradicate. Waves of immigration have enriched and, in some cases, led to the development of whole areas. Once derelict streets have become home to vibrant artistic communities. In short the area continues to change and grow yet somehow remain fiercely itself. Community is a word which is much bandied around, but no single community exists; as in all major Cities community is a patchwork of diverse hues. Bethnal Green is composed of a variety of peoples of differing races, creeds and colours some of whom get along together and some of whom do not. It is not the object of this book to peddle and support any myth, but to

Corner of Warner Place and
Hackney Road 1900

look at a distinct area of Bethnal Green known as The Jesus Hospital Estate. This small pocket of land has a rich history going back over three hundred years. Surprisingly, in these days of constant movement and agitation, some descendants of the first inhabitants of the Estate still live in the very houses to which their forebears came back in the mid 1800s.

It is this shared history which forms the substance of this book. This is not an exhaustive, or academic, study of an area but a series of "snapshots" of times past and times present from an area which, despite all remains stubbornly and resolutely unique.

Bethnal Green Road at the junction with Brick Lane looking eastwards, 1905

IN THE BEGINNING

BEFORE MAN CAME TO THE AREA NOW
KNOWN AS BETHNAL GREEN THE LAND
WAS A MIXTURE OF MARSHLAND AND FOREST
OVERLYING THE RIVER TERRACE GRAVELS OF
THE THAMES.

These gravels in turn sit upon rich London clay. The area was probably occupied in the Iron age as a coin of that period was found near an ancient roadway through Victoria Park[1]. Saxon beads found during an excavation in Brick Lane are firm evidence of settlement at that time[2]. The place name Blithehale or Blythenhale, the earliest form of Bethnal Green, is from the Anglo-Saxon healh 'angle, nook or corner' and blithe 'happy' or possibly from a personal name Blitha[3].

The first clearance of land and establishment of a settlement was in the area which is now home to Bethnal Green's Museum of Childhood. At the back of this lay St Winifred's well which was the source of water for the village during in 12th and 13th centuries[4]. Bethnal Green emerged from obscurity as a setting for a ballad which was dramatised in 1600 and later embellished.

It is the story of a blinded soldier named Montfort, rescued by a woman with whom he lived as a beggar on Bethnal Green. Myth would have it that the man was Simon de Montfort's son Henry who was killed at the battle of Evesham in 1265[5]. The play of 1600 showed evidence of much local knowledge and by the 17th century the legend was well established with an inn, the Blind Beggar of Bethnal Green (built 1654) with the beggars dwelling preserved nearby. Centuries later the descendant of that inn was to be the site of one of the murders associated with the Kray Twins[6].

Although at first inhabited by a predominantly peasant community, the area attracted its fair share of notables seeking a country retreat from the rigours of City life. They built large houses mostly around the Green itself and there are descriptions of lavish parties and much "amusement". A roll call from the 16th century includes Lord Powis, The Lord Mayor of London Sir Richard Gresham, Sir John Gates chancellor of the Duchy of Lancaster and, perhaps hinting at a later association with neer do wells, Robert Catesby the Gunpowder conspirator who was known to have lived 'in an out-place in Bethnal Green'[7].

By the early 17th century Bethnal Green had a proportionally larger middle class population than any of the Stepney hamlets with the exception of Mile End on the edge of the City of London itself[8].

Samuel Pepys, the great diarist, was much taken with the area where he was able to find "cream and good cherries"[9]. So safe a haven did he feel it to be that he fled here during the Great Fire of London

Original plan of the Jesus Hospital Estate

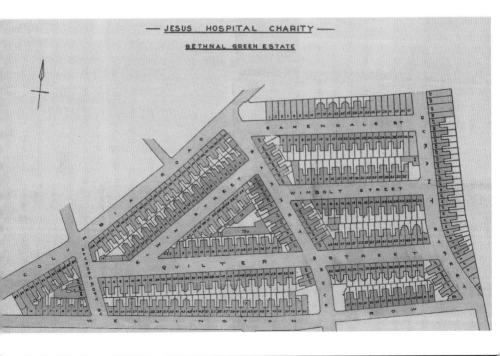

of 1666 [10] bringing his great works with him.

Like much of London the land in Bethnal Green was developed in a spasmodic way with no street plan or overriding concept for the area. As a consequence of this, and the parallel development of London westwards towards Mayfair and Chelsea, poorer tenant farmers became the predominant inhabitants of the area as the gentry sought their pleasures elsewhere.

OUR STORY BEGINS IN THE THIRTY NINTH YEAR OF THE REIGN OF QUEEN ELIZABETH I WHEN ONE JAMES RAVENSCROFT, AN UPSTANDING CHURCHMAN OF HERTFORDSHIRE, FOUNDED JESUS HOSPITAL (CHARITY) IN CHIPPING BARNET EXPRESSLY TO PROVIDE THE ACCOMMODATION 'OF SIX POOR AND ANCIENT …' THE DATE 28TH APRIL 1679.

Guinness trust buildings today, the car park to the right is where the bomb fell

THE

ESTATE

1679 —————————————— 1863

In the deeds of the establishment
of the charity it is stated that

JAMES RAVENSCROFT

granted to the charity,

*'the greatest part of a certain
close in stepney at Stebonheath
in the county of Middlesex.'*

As Bethnal Green was one of the hamlets of
Stepney this land was, and still is,

THE JESUS HOSPITAL ESTATE
OF BETHNAL GREEN.

exactly how James Ravenscroft came to be
in possession of this land is not known.

Interior of hospital ward in France where Thomas Mitchell was treated in 1916

Given the stature of some of the tenants of Bethnal Green village in the 17th century it is entirely likely that he had passed through the area on his way along Hackney Road when visiting colleagues or friends. Until well after 1700 Hackney Road was devoid of buildings on its south side hence the farmland would have been visible from the road[11].

This must remain conjecture however. What we do know is that in 1679 all that was on this land was a farmhouse and outbuildings at the eastern end of Crabtree Lane (Columbia Road) at the junction of a field way (Gibraltar Walk). It was in the tenure of one Robert Newell, yeoman, at a rent of £34 per annum.

Over the years certain of the Visitors from the Charity were to rue the bequest of this land. As Visitors they were unpaid volunteers but had the "Superintendence, Rule and Government (of Jesus Hospital) …and all of the Revenue and affairs thereof."

The first group of Visitors resided in Barnet, thereafter the Deed especially dictated that they should not be local to that area in order, one supposes, to avoid corruption. The Bethnal Green estate was distant from the Charity's other properties the majority of which were in South Hertfordshire or Essex. From what transpired it is unlikely that any of the Visitors were local to East London, or even knew where Bethnal Green was.

Apart from a prosaic drawing of the Jesus Hospital Estate from 1689, the Charity itself reports little of note until 1822 when they decided to develop the area for housing.

By 1822 the southern area of Hackney Road had been built upon. The Birdcage Public House had made an appearance on the corner of the Jesus Hospital Estate as

early as 1760 where it had replaced the original farmhouse of Robert Newell. The land though remained virtually empty with only three further dwellings erected between 1760 and 1822.

With the expansion of the docks and industry, pressure to provide suitable accommodation for the burgeoning working classes was growing. Urban deprivation was already a reality and bubonic plague, typhoid, TB and latterly Cholera were synonymous with the area. The area by St Katherine's by the Tower of London was particularly infamous for its overcrowding and desperate conditions with up to forty families using one toilet. The water supply was equally insufficient being via standpipes which were turned on or off at the whim of the Water Companies.

It was the desire of the Charity to erect dwellings in keeping with a more civilised lifestyle. The Estate was already bordered by ill constructed weavers cottages and the Visitors were desirous to create something more durable.

The plan (*page 11*) shows the layout of the Estate pretty much as it is today;

Map of the area, 1845

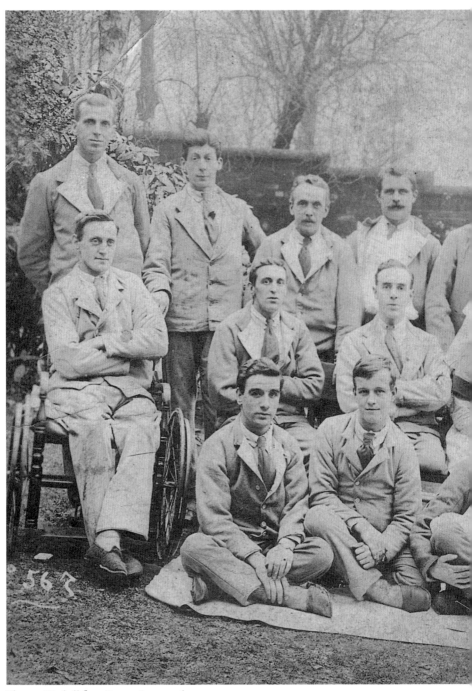

Thomas Mitchell from Durant Street to the
right of the nurse, France 1916

Outside the bakery in Barnet Grove, 1910

the tale of its building however, is living proof that jerry builders are no new phenomenon. We tend think that "they built things well in the old days". They might have, but they didn't on this estate and it is a miracle that the houses still stand to this day.

The landscape in the early nineteenth century was a far cry from the countryside which Pepys had so lovingly described.

Maps are notoriously unreliable at this period but the map from 1845 (*page 16*) will prove to illustrate the point. As you can see the land to the north and east of the map is still Middlesex farmland. In the built up areas there are still a few pockets of open space. The area which concerns us is that bounded by Crabtree Row, Wellington Row and the western side of Edith Place. The whole landscape apart from the farmland of Jesus Hospital Estate was, by this time, pock marked with excavation sites and the air polluted with the belch of fumes from kilns. Deep pits lay water filled where builders had burrowed down to find the London clay from which to make the bricks to construct the houses.

The gravel which overlay this was piled high behind the pits where it was often used as an ancillary refuse dump by the locals. General sanitation was rudimentary to say the least; the main sewer which served the East End near Mile End was open to the elements and was a wide river of filth.

THE LAND WHICH COMPRISED

THE JESUS
HOSPITAL ESTATE

HAD ONCE BEEN KNOWN FOR PRODUCING

A CROP WHICH ONLY GROWS
IN THE PUREST OF AIR AND WATER,

ONE DOUBTS AT THIS POINT THAT ANY SUCH WHOLESOME
COMMODITIES WERE STILL TO BE FOUND.

If the account produced by the Charity is true, and there is no reason to suppose otherwise, it took forty one years to bring their housing plan to fruition. On the 16th November 1822 the Visitors put the responsibility for developing the Estate into the hands of a Mr Robert Abraham, surveyor of Torrington Street Middlesex and Mr Quilter, Visitor and the Charity's Solicitor. One can only assume that the Visitors were a well meaning but naive group of people, for what ensued resembles a Carry On farce. Although given the debacles of the Greenwich Dome and the New Tate Bridge not much seems to have changed on that score. Mr Abraham appeared out of nowhere, he is never minuted as attending any of the Charity's prior meetings, and one might assume that he had heard about the proposed development and

made a direct approach. Whatever the mechanism, on Lady Day (March 25) 1823 possession of the land was obtained from the farmer following which Mr Abraham submitted his plan for the "proposed building and arrangement of the streets" together with an offer from a Mr Abbott for a building lease for a term of 42 years, set at an annual rent of £400.

Had the Visitors remained true to the original Deed as set out by James Ravenscroft they would have saved themselves a lot of aggravation. It was explicit that the Visitors should not hold lands which exceeded an annual rent of £200. Finding a way around this they granted Mr Abbot his request.

Warning bells should have sounded when the gentleman in question then decided that it would not be in his interest to sign the lease. The Visitors for reasons best known to themselves acceded and Mr Abbot began work without the liability of lease or contract.

He finally signed the lease but took little note of its terms. Brick quarries abounded in the locality so it had seemed unnecessary for him to quarry on the Estate's land; ignoring this he proceeded to turn the pasture land into yet another moonscape. Rent remained unpaid and finally when the properties were inspected they were deemed unsuitable for habitation. In addition, he had indulged in that well known pass time of sub-letting so that not only he, but a number of others had to be turfed off the land, but how to do it?

If the Visitors had one skill it was an ability to use the legal system. In the original Deed Visitors were not empowered to grant a lease in excess of 21 years. This was reinforced by Statute 39 raised during the reign of Elizabeth I under which the Charity had been founded.

So in 1828 the Charity was once more in possession of the land with its attendant groupings of dilapidated buildings. The sole building of note was the previously mentioned Birdcage Public house built by the brewery Messrs. Combe and Delafield who leased the land from the Estate.

In 1827 Mr Thomas Henry Elwin a Rector of East Barnet became a Visitor to the Charity and rapidly rose to the rank of Chairman. It was he, and Mr Quilter, who bore the brunt of the frustrations which the Bethnal Green Estate would continue to bring them until 1862.

After the first debacle the Charity had no funds to pay Mr Abraham or Mr Quilter. This distressed financial situation required drastic action and they rapidly agreed a proposal put to them by one Mr Bourne. On the face of it all looked well, the lease granted to Mr Bourne was for the proscribed 21 yrs, the rent though was rather low £45 for the first year rising to a maximum of £90 with a further payment of 12.5 pence (2/6d) per thousand bricks produced from quarrying.

The first batch of houses built, once again before a lease was signed, were of such poor quality that they had to be demolished before that lease was duly executed. One would have thought that a modicum of suspicion might have crept into the Visitors minds at this point. If it did there is no evidence of it, for in 1834 Mr Bourne surrendered his lease and took out a further lease for the maximum 21 yrs. This process was to continue so that by the time Mr Bourne died in 1843 his wife, now the lessee, was in possession of the land until 1860. She fully intended to seek a further extension on the grounds that a great deal of money had been spent on building houses and that Mr Bourne had been involved in "numberless disputes and litigation with vexatious and unprincipled parties".

At this point somebody descended from the giddy heights of Barnet and went and had a look at what had been built. They found that houses had been erected without due notice to the Charity's surveyor and that they were smaller in scale than agreed. As before, workmanship was of a very poor quality and the drainage was completely insufficient. It was notable that the surveyor Mr Abraham had not instigated any system for the completion of any one street or line of houses. A map of the area in 1862 shows that only Barnet Grove was a complete street. Mrs Bourne was not granted an extension to her lease and once more in 1861 the Charity took back possession of the land. At this time 182 houses had been constructed, two thirds of them were of only one story and many so badly built that they were "worn out".

The only good thing to arise from this particular endeavour was that the Charity's financial position was temporarily eased in that the rents previously paid to Mrs Bourne now came to them in the order of the princely sum of £540 per annum.

Logic should have told the Visitors than nobody would have erected substantial dwellings on a lease of only 21 yrs. The whole estate was now a slum with open sewage running along channels beside the roads.

A snapshot of the conditions which prevailed in the area can be obtained from the wonderfully titled "Sanitary Ramblings" written by Dr Hector Gavin, lecturer in forensic medicine at Charing Cross Hospital who betook it upon himself to inspect the conditions in the slums of East London[12]. The book was published in 1848 at which point he mentions two streets on the Estate Wellington Row and Barnet Grove. Interestingly Barnet Grove does not appear on the 1845 map but Gavin States that;

"BARNET GROVE *crossed the centre of the Estate* (JESUS HOSPITAL) *by 1845,*

having 31 houses by 1846."

OF THE CONDITIONS HE WRITES;

"BARNET GROVE IS ALWAYS *remarkably dirty;* THE HOUSES ARE DAMP, MANY OF THEM BEING IN SMALL GARDENS."

Walking southwards he finds:

"WELLINGTON ROW—

A STREET ENTIRELY OCCUPIED BY WEAVERS,

THE STREET ITSELF

IS VERY DIRTY

AND THE GUTTERS FULL;

THE HOUSES ARE THE USUAL

CONSTRUCTION OF WEAVERS HOUSES

AND OF COURSE GREATLY

DEFECTIVE AS REGARDS

VENTILATION.

THE NORTHERN SIDE OF THE STREET

(the Estate side)

CONSISTS OF COTTAGES AND GARDENS

WHICH ARE

GENERALLY NEATLY LAID OUT."

This last statement may support some of the local stories about the building of the houses. Wellington Row is said to be much older than the rest of the Estate. If these houses were in good order it is possible that they were not torn down in the next round of building. Local lore has it that Wellington Row was built in 1845/7. If true this would also explain why the general structure of the houses seems to be of the type of those built in a period before the 1860s. Perhaps the final builder of the Estate decided to leave these houses in place and follow the earlier style. It is notable that those lowly weavers houses to which Gavin alludes were only pulled down in 1941 (personal testimony) so it is very likely that the Wellington Row houses were left unmolested.

Whatever the truth the present estate owes its existence to the Charity Act of 1853. This had lead to the appointment of the Board of Charity Commissioners to assist, control and advise charities in carrying out their various functions.

Although Mr Abraham, having died in 1851, had been spectacularly unsuccessful in his dealings with the Charity, his son was appointed as Charity surveyor to oversee the third attempt at building the houses. Did the Visitors hear any warning bells this time? True, he was another individual but Henry Robert Abraham would surely have known how much wool could be pulled over eyes. However, any submission to build now had to be approved by an entirely independent surveyor. This was duly done and in 1862 Mr George Clarkson of 9a Great St Helens, Bishopsgate Street, London E.C., was leased the land for 60 years.

Over the period of the next few years 372 properties to house Londoners were erected on the site. A shopping arcade on Columbia Road was built and several public houses to provide entertainment for the local populace.

The Charity continued to administer the Estate until 1979; in all three hundred years of unbroken patronage.

left: *Wellington Row*
as it is today

1860 — 1900

So, who were the first inhabitants of the houses on the Estate and how did they live? As so often with social history that which is written by visitors, the "foreigners", who scoured the East End to view its squalor, differs markedly from the stories told by the locals.

In "Ragged London" written in 1861 by John Hollingshead[13], the inhabitants of the broader Bethnal Green are "mainly poor dock labourers, poor costermongers, poor silk-weavers, clinging hopelessly to a withering handicraft, the lowest kind of thieves, the most ill disguised class of swell mobsmen with a sprinkling of box and toy makers, shoe makers and cheap cabinet makers. Its women are mainly hawkers, sempstresses, the coarsest order of prostitutes, and aged stall keepers."

Mr Hollinghead's text goes on to describe a society of cheap eating houses, musty dens, faded grocers etc.. every adjective is pejorative. The object of his discourse, no doubt, was to engender philanthropic interest in this part of London but by its very nature the work defines the inhabitants of the area as somehow less than human.

Ten years later in 1871 in the periodical, The Builder[14], Crabtree Row (Columbia Road) is described thus, "we had to pick our way through six inches of heavy sludge…Here we find poverty, dirt and rags. No scraper or besom (bunch of twigs for sweeping) sweeps in here, nor are the denizens alive to the danger that surrounds them. Their homes are grave and bare and the gravest

right: *Columbia Market, 1914;*
following spread: *Exterior of Columbia Market as originally conceived*

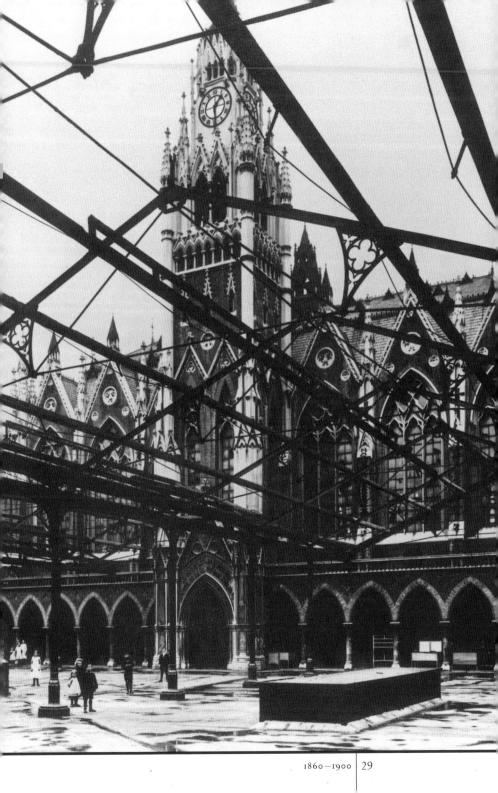

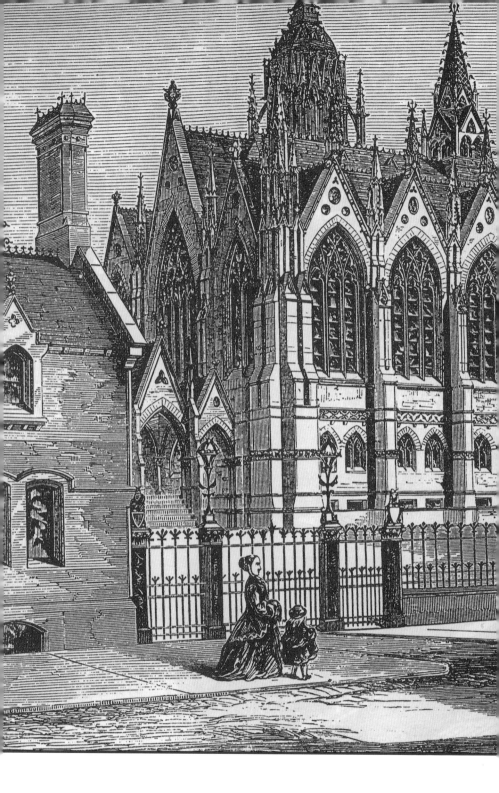

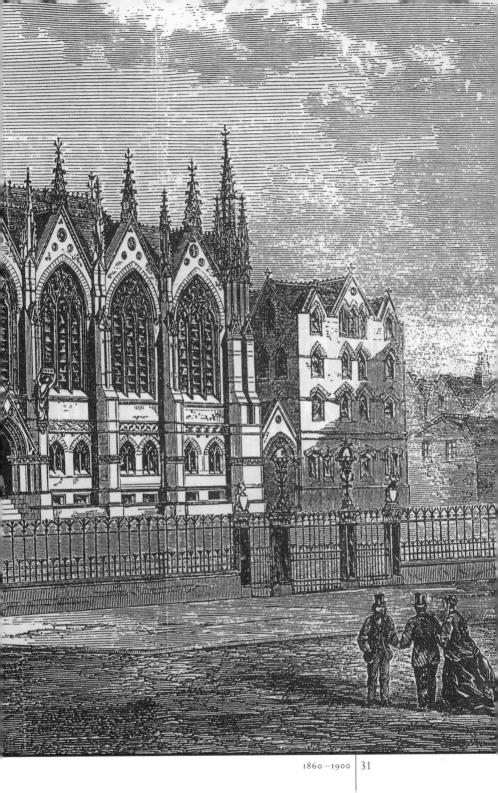

concern of their lives is how they will be able to "make both ends meet", by Saturday night. We move along through a narrow passageway and while thinking what a villainous spot this would be on a dark night, find we are safely emerging into Virginia Row."

So, poor and dangerous and filled with smelly, uneducated people? Whatever the truth of the matter this image promulgated by the Victorians has remained, more or less intact, up to the present day but was it the whole picture?

An inkling that this supposed morass of illiterates were a breed apart, and not a very grateful breed at that, came with Angela Burdett Coutts spectacular Columbia Market on Columbia Road, the site of which is now occupied by the high rise of Sivill House and the surrounding maisonettes of the 1960s.

At the time in which the gentlemen from The Builder were risking their lives in visiting the area this neo Gothic pile (*pages 30-31*), which much resembled St Pancras Station, was already standing empty. Persuaded by Charles Dickens that the local costermongers would be better served by working indoors Baroness Coutts had this ill fated phoenix erected; but for once Mr Dickens had read his cards wrong.

The misguided Baroness, having already facilitated the renaming of Crabtree Row as Columbia Road in honour of the Bishopric of British Columbia which she had recently founded, now sought to use religion to tame the wild costermongers of the East End.

IT WAS AN INSTANT
FAILURE. SHADY DEALS
WERE BETTER SUITED TO
SHADY STREET CORNERS
AND THE TRADERS AVOIDED
THE PRETENTIOUS MARKET
LIKE THE PLAGUE.

Extract from the 1891 census.

CON-DITION as to Marriage	AGE last Birthday of (Males / Females)	PROFESSION or OCCUPATION	Employer	Employed	Neither Employer nor Employed	WHERE BORN		If (1) Deaf-and-Dumb (2) Blind (3) Lanatic, Imbecile or Idiot
M	X	Linsed Victualler Pub	X	—	—	London	Camden Town	
M	34					Norfolk	Gt Yarmouth	
	6	Scholar				Essex	Carrying Town	
	X	do				London	Shoreditch	
		do						
Widow	34	Housekeeper Dom			X	Norfolk	Gt Yarmouth	
Single	29	No occupation						
S	24 24	Barman			X	Surrey	Lambeth	
S	22 22	do	Dom		X	Essex	Grays	
do	18 18	do			X	Stafford	Walsall	
M	35	Grocer	X			Somerset	Bristol	
M	32					London	Shoreditch	
	X	Scholar				do	Kings Cross	
S	16	General Servant Dom				do	Shadwell	
M	39	Iron Merchant	X			London	Bethnal Green	
M	34					do	do	
	3					do	do	
	X					do	do	
S	X	General Servant Dom				Kent	Bracklee	
Widow	46	Ironmonger			X	London	Spitalfields	
S	24	Fancy Box Maker Paper B	X			do	Bethnal Green	
S	20	do	X			do	do	
S	14	Fancy Box Maker Neither I	X			do	do	
S	14	Scholar Fancy Box Maker Paper X B				do	do	
	X	Scholar				do	do	
	X	do				do	do	
M	34	Commercial Clerk			X	do	do	
M	34					do	do	
	10	Scholar				do	do	
Widow	45	Fealse Washer				do	Cripplegate	
S	18	Porter				do	St Lukes	
Females...	13 / 18							1891

What many of these well-meaning people missed was the fact that there was a community here and one which had its own way of operating. There were areas of terrible deprivation that was true, but there were also areas of lesser poverty in which most people were employed and where ends indeed could meet. Reading the transcripts of the time, whilst coming from the area myself, it is yawningly obvious that it was all a matter of relativity. I am sure that to Frederick Charrington, George Peabody and other purveyors of philanthropy the whole East End was a black, disease infested pit. But you didn't have to look far to realise that this was not the case, even poverty had its genteel side.

IT IS SAID THAT THE COSTERMONGERS WHO BRIEFLY INHABITED THE MARKET WERE THOSE WHO FOUNDED WHAT HAS BECOME COLUMBIA ROAD FLOWER MARKET. ANECDOTAL EVIDENCE FROM MY GRANDMOTHER, ALICE, TELLS ANOTHER STORY. MANY YEARS AGO SHE TOLD ME THAT COLUMBIA ROAD HAD BEEN CRABTREE ROW, BARNET ST, BIRDCAGE WALK AND, SHE ASSURED ME, BEFORE THAT SHEEP ROW. SUPPOSEDLY IT WAS PART OF THE ROUTE ALONG WHICH SHEEP WERE WALKED ON THEIR WAY TO THE SLAUGHTERHOUSES AT SMITHFIELD. THE MARKET GARDENERS OF THE AREA BEGAN SELLING THEIR PRODUCE ON THE EDGES OF THIS WELL DEFINED WALK-WAY A VERY LONG TIME AGO. AS URBANISATION OVERTOOK THE AREA THIS REMNANT OF A RURAL PAST REMAINED AND EVOLVED INTO THE MARKET WHICH IS THERE TODAY.

Before turning to the recollections of those whose parents and grandparents lived in the area it is worthwhile taking a look at the 1891 census.

I am going to concentrate on Columbia Road as it is representative of the inhabitants of much of the Estate plus it has the shops which can be charted through the years.

Firstly let me describe the interior of the buildings on Columbia Road. This is a description of the south side which forms part of the Jesus Hospital Estate. My aunts had a haberdashers shop at 152 Columbia Road which hadn't been altered since the properties were built with the exception, I suspect, that the house had its own cold water supply.

The shop area had a work room behind it the whole area would be about 20 feet by 15 at the most. The living area was three rooms upstairs, a kitchen and tiny scullery downstairs and a toilet out back with a cold water supply to the scullery. There are very small backyards.

In 1891 the professions of the inhabitants were pretty much as described by our wandering philanthropists. I cannot attest to the quality of the prostitutes or the depravity of the criminals but in so far as defined professions go they were accurate.

As with earlier censuses examined (1841-1871) the majority of inhabitants were born locally either in Bethnal Green, Shoreditch, Spitalfields or Mile End. There are some individuals from Norfolk, York and some of the southern counties but these are few. Europe is represented by only three families. Firstly at number 132 (now Columbia Pottery) was John Roshett the head of the family who ran a hairdressers who was Swiss; at 156 (now Atelier) lived Hermann Reitig from Germany, age 53, who was an Umbrella stick maker; and at 162 (now the corner shop) was another German, Frederick Schneider, age 30, who was a Pork Butcher. A long tradition of Welsh Dairymen was in evidence with David Jones age thirty six from Cardiganshire at 216 (now demolished) whose whole family is bracketed in the census with the single word Milk written next to it. Cheese was provided by the Irish in the guise of Archibald Freu age 31 at 142 (now Symonds).

The Roshett family, of two individuals, occupied the whole downstairs of the house with the three member Kelsey family, who were bootmakers, occupying the two rooms upstairs. The five Reitigs occupied the whole of 156 as did the five Schneiders in 162. These professionals lived in relative luxury in comparison to the cabinet makers, general domestic servants, errand boys, weavers, railway workers, laundresses, boot makers and house cleaners.

In the rooms which you occupied you ate, slept and washed, there was a single privy out in the back yard and a pump nearby from which you got water.

The more general rule for the street was up to ten people living in the accommodation set aside for occupancy. Hence at 132, four member of the Jacobs family (mattress maker and boot machinist) lived in three rooms; Richard Rawles and his wife Amelia (domestic servant and packing crate maker) in two;

and the Baldry family of three (carman and boot machinist) in one- total nine. The majority of the properties were divided up thus. Even the Medical practitioner Francis Warwick's household at 146 (now Marcos and Trump) comprised nine people; him, his wife five daughters and lodgers Mr and Mrs Turner (B Clicker boot trade and laundress wash).

What is notable is that the great Jewish diaspora stopped short of crossing Bethnal Green Road and entering this part of East London. Later a small Jewish Community was in existence in Ravenscroft Buildings (now demolished) but in 1891 with the exceptions of the Jacobs family and the Kelseys there is no evidence of anybody with recognisably Jewish names.

Somehow the presence of Pork Butchers, Hairdressers, Grocers shops, Medical Practitioners and Corn Chandlers doesn't quite fit with the descriptions of abject squalor applied to the area. Ten years earlier the census of 1881 revealed that Columbia Road was as full of shops and trades as it was in 1891.

In Charles Booth's great Descriptive Map of London Poverty of 1889 the Estate is coloured pink, defined as: "Working-class comfort (F but with some G)". G was defined as some households having one or two servants. Indeed a stone's throw away at the end of Baxendale Street in Ion Square the 1851 census reveals three teachers a doctor, a dentist and a local minister living in the square as well as cabinet makers, milliners and boot binders. Five families were shown to have a servant.

What was the area really like?

Bethnal Green Road, 1903

EARLIEST

memories

TO THE ———————— 1930S

"My grandfather lived at number 23 Elwin Street. He was Tommy Orange, the famous bare-fist fighter, and he put this area on the map. He had a stupendous funeral (1937) we still take the relatives from Australia over to see where he's buried (in Manor Park). He must have been a protestant, Tommy Orange, because his real name was Cochrane."

Woven post card sent by Thomas Mitchell from the front, circa 1916

Ethel Zebedee was born in 1919 and has always lived in either Elwin or Quilter Street. Given the disputes about the timing of the building of the Estate I am leaving her dates for her grandparents first occupancy as given. Ethel's family's story:

E: "MY GRANDPARENTS WERE THE FIRST ONES IN THEIR HOUSE AND I THINK IT WAS EITHER 1857 OR 1859 AND THEY HAD 14 KIDS. WHEN THEY MOVED IN THERE WAS AN OPEN FIRE IN THE KITCHEN AND A HOOK. YOU COOKED MEAT BY PUTTING IT ON THE HOOK AND THE FAT WOULD DRIP INTO A DISH. I CAN REMEMBER THAT. THEY ALWAYS PUT SOMETHING UP TO STOP ME TOUCHING THE FIRE. NOT LONG AFTER THEY MOVED IN THEY HAD CANDLES REPLACED BY GAS.

Between fights my grandpa used to take grandma to Paris. When she had a baby they'd leave the older ones to look after it. He'd give her the money to go to Tottenham Court Road and she used to walk to her favourite Milliners and have a hat made then go over to Paris for a long weekend. Famous people used to come down here to see him. Charles Buchanan from the Daily Express; grandpa was in all the papers. People thought the Krays funeral was grand, it was nothing compared to his. He used to fight for a purse and a scarf. He died in 1937. In 1938 we had an idea war was coming we had a practice blackout. We all said, 'Thank god grandpa's gone. He'd have shipped us all out of the country.'

Especially us (her siblings) because my dad died when he was 36, I was seven and my young sister was five so grandpa looked out for us. My dad died of pneumonia, ridiculous. It only took 3 days. They'd brought him back from France 3 times with pneumonia. The last time they took him to Swindon. The soldiers took my mother to see him but he died. I always understood it was pneumonia. There was no State money then so the family kept her.

L: *She didn't remarry?*

E: *No, who's going to marry a woman with three young kids? She did meet somebody because she finished up with a rather good job at the Stock Exchange. We kids thought it was wonderful, we had an Uncle George. But my grandmother said to her how do you know he's going to love your kids like you want him to? She put dubious thoughts in Mum's mind so she never remarried.*

Mum always worked; She'd leave us three kids in bed. My elder sister was seven years older than me. Mum had lost a son between the two of us, it was because of the war (WW1) you know. She left the house at 5.45. Often she used to walk because she couldn't afford the penny fare. She's leave all of our breakfasts with all of our names on. She always got back in time to see us off to school.

Syd Longcroft's aunt and her family were living upstairs in our house at this point (26 Elwin). I was born in 10 Elwin, we moved to number 26 when I was six weeks old then to this house (in Quilter Street) when I was twenty and have been here for the last sixty years.

You never thought of moving out of the area. You had to be really comfortable to think of moving out of the area. Aunty Jenny who had the corner shop did well and moved to Mildmay Park, Dalston, but when she moved to Highams Park we thought she'd really outdone herself. We used to love visiting her up there.

Most of the Aunt's moved away but some stayed. One lived in the Crescent at the end of Columbia Road near where Barbara Windsor's mum and grandparents lived. Crescent place was full of funny little houses, it was where Cuff Point is now, opposite Leopold Buildings (western end of Columbia Road). In amongst the houses were shops, there was Fitz-Hughes the grocers and Thomas's the dairy. It was a real maze. When the war (WW1) came my aunt and uncle moved to Chingford.

Uncle Albert was shot while they were signing the Armistice in WW1. My grandma and grandpa went to St Pauls Cathedral and were presented with a silver chain. My grandmother had it on her handbag. Two babies (of my grandparents) were lost, they died of Diphtheria.

left: *Mr and Mrs Cuff, founders of the Shoreditch Tabernacle, circa 1880;* right: *Ethel Zebedee*

*The Jolly Boy's outing from the
Royal Oak Pub, 1930s*

IN THOSE DAYS PEOPLE WITH DIPHTHERIA

HAD TO GO TO LONDON BRIDGE,

get on a barge and were taken up river.

WHEN THEY LANDED THEY HAD TO PUT ON

CLOAKS LIKE MONKS

and were put in isolation at Dartford.

When Tommy, grandpa, came out of the fighting business he worked in the sawmills in Virginia Road, but he had all his contacts all the same.

We all used to play together in the streets then, even the adults, the men used to hold a skipping rope, it was a village atmosphere round here, it really was. We especially loved playing on the Asphalt.

The Asphalt? That was between Columbia, Ravenscroft and Gossett Streets it was the first time Asphalt was ever used anywhere in the country. It was tested there we used it as our skating rink.

Shopping was a different thing altogether too. Hobb's oil shop was on the corner where the Chemist is now (104 Columbia). You could buy a pennyworth of jam or pickles. You took your cup round, nobody bought jars. You took your jug for fresh milk. There were two deliveries of milk a day once early then at eleven in the morning with Pudding Milk for your afters, or sweet as they say today. We had a safe out the back yard with perforated metal on three sides. The back was covered so your neighbour couldn't see what you'd got."

Although Tommy Orange might not have been your typical East Ender the life which Ethel describes seems pretty much true of the area as a whole. Her grandfather had a level of affluence which many others did not but nonetheless life, although tough, doesn't seem to have been intolerable.

A theme which emerged early on in the interviews was the tendency for people to stick to their own streets. People who were interviewed who grew up on Durant Street only knew people from say Elwin Street, some three streets away, by sight. For the older generation this very much carries through into the present day. There were so many children in each street you didn't have to look far for playmates and by the time you went to work your circle of friends was well defined. Ethel Zebedee and Albert Lewis were born in the same year within a few doors of one another. Albert's family was involved in the furniture trade which dominated the area until the 1960s. Theresa, Albert's wife, came from a family of butchers who had a shop on Columbia Road. Albert Lewis recalling the 1920s on Columbia Road

"If you wanted new laid eggs you got them from Barnards the Chemist on Columbia Road

cal shopping guide, 1920s

(number 84). *They were in a small box with sawdust and guaranteed laid that day. You could have them say if you were sick or you had just had a baby. Next door to there at number 82 was Bendons the grocers; that was Watsons in the 1920s they did the same kind of groceries. Then you came to the Birdcage Pub.*

Nate Joel had the pub in the 1920s; but it was in the family. His father had it before him. Nate's dad, Harry Joel, was the original landlord in the current Birdcage pub. Harry got thrown out of the West End because he used to grass on the villains who came into his pub up there. The police got him out of the West End and found the Birdcage for him.

Underneath the Red Buildings were some shops. The one on the corner sold haberdashery, it was always something and three farthings. Next to that was a Jewish grocers then you had the buildings. Also in the 1920s was Freemans a Jewish shop. They sold men's long pants and women's underwear, fleecy lined knickers with the elastic around them, bloomers. They sold combinations for men to wear in the winter.

Morgan's the dairy was where the Tapas bar is now 93. Mr Morgan used to come around with the trolley and take the milk out of the urn. We used to have tankards with a lid on hanging on a nail out outside your house. Mr Morgan would come along and fill it up and

hang it up for you to pick up later."

"I (Albert) was born in this house and my father was born here too. My father was a French polisher like me. We had a little shop in Ravenscroft Street. 15/- (75p) a week it cost to rent. We packed up and moved to Gibraltar Walk when we found a place for 12/- (60p) a week. We put all our gear on the barrow and off we went. I was born in 1919 and dad was born in 1887. Dad's family came from round the corner near the oil shop (104 Columbia Road). Grandmother had a goat in her back yard and my father had a goat in the back yard here. When Grandmother used to go up West on the hawk she had a pony and cart and she used to bring the pony through the passage and park him through in the back yard. When this house was done up in the early 1980s they dug the yard up and found the pony's hoof and skull. We always wondered what happened to it.

I think I must have Jewish blood as many took the name. My mother's single name was Marks she came from Plaistow. My grandmother, my father's mother, her single name was Isaacs. "

"On the hawk" was when you went around knocking on peoples doors and asking for their unwanted goods, this was usually clothes. Albert's mum was well known for this in the area. Between their two families, Albert and Theresa, embody

previous spread: *(left to right)*
Albert Lewis, Gladys Herd and
Theresa Lewis;
left: *Former furniture factory*
on Columbia Road

much of the ethnic and professional mix of people who first lived on the Estate.

Theresa: "*My mother was a French Hugenot, I've got Irish blood in me on mum's side too. My father's side was all rank Irish. My mother's name was Fobbester. And they all settled down Old Ford. Mum was a silk weaver, she used to do some beautiful crocheting. When she died I still found the ball* (of silk) *with a crochet hook in it and beautiful lace doyleys.*"

Albert on female French Polishers:

"*Next door to where Ethel Zebedee lives now was old mother Gardner, she used to do* (polish) *chairs in her kitchen. Next door but one was the Dix's whose mother used to polish chairs on the table. Mrs McQueen in Quilter Street was another polisher. They were relations to the Dents who lived in Columbia Road. Mrs McQueen and Mrs Dent were sisters and they were both polishers. There weren't many Hugenots this side then they were all towards Old Ford.*"

The wood industry dominated the area from the 1840s up until the 1970s. In the period between 1839 and 1850 two hundred miles of new streets were built in Metropolitan London and upon those streets were constructed 6,405 new dwellings some, if not all of which, needed furniture.

Very little furniture had been built in East London before that time, the majority having been made in a series of workshops which stretched between St Pauls in the City and Aldersgate. With the need for more, and cheaper, furniture a generally smaller, fragmented, industry grew up which often involved all of the members of a family.

All aspects of the trade were under-taken in the area and, as Albert has indicated, women played their part. The 1881 census reveals that there were 248 female French Polishers working in the East End.

Evidence of that industry is still with us today. On Columbia Road there are two former factories, one still with Raven Furniture displayed on the front of the building. The second near the Royal Oak Pub was Davenports a firm which assembled the final product. Signs such as one in Ezra Street attest to this recently demised past.

Wood was milled in a variety of places, one of the largest of these mills being in Ezra Street courtyard, with many smaller mills and turners dotted around on streets such as Wimbolt and Durant. The various parts were then processed. Chair and table legs were taken by cart to the wood carvers who then passed them on to the assemblers who then passed them on to the veneerers and polishers, many of whom as has already been described, worked from home. An almost constant stream of half assembled furniture was always being trundled through the streets. Recently, after a period of a few years with no local wood industry, a small industrial unit handling mostly medium density fibre board had opened on Durant Street.

Marie Stephens grew up in Guinness Buildings. Her mother's family were Hugenots and had come from Normandy in the 1600s. Her father's family lived on Fleet Street Hill near Brick Lane before the railway was built in the 1840s, they were Irish.

MARIE STEPHENS ON STREET TRADING:
"FOOD FOR SALE ON THE STREETS WAS
VERY SEASONAL, OUTSIDE THE BIRDCAGE PUB
THERE USED TO BE A MAN WHO SOLD BAKED
POTATOES FOR A PENNY WHICH HE BAKED ON
A BRAZIER. OUTSIDE GUINNESS BUILDINGS
A MR MONKSFIELD USED TO SELL ICE-CREAM
AND FROZEN CUSTARD. IN THE SUMMER
OUTSIDE THE GLOBE PUB (NOW STRINGRAY
PIZZERIA) WAS A BARROW COVERED IN A PURE
WHITE SHEET WHICH SOLD PIGS TROTTERS,
ALL STEAMED. 1D HALF, 2D WHOLE. WE USED
TO PUT VINEGAR ON THEM."

The Herd children and their playmates in Cadell Street, 1930s

*Thomas Mitchell taking a group
out on a Beano*

Vinegar is a way of life around here. We put it on eggs, bacon, jellied eels. There are many theories as to why it is used. Perhaps it was to mask the taste of rancid food, perhaps a hang over from a Hugenot past in which vinegar, or lemons, were used in cooking.

Marie again.

"Also there was a hawker who used to come into Guinness Buildings; although they weren't supposed to. He was an Indian and he was the only Indian we knew. He used to have a biscuit tin tied around his neck and he rang a bell. He sold "Indian Toffee". It was like candy floss sold on a newspaper cornet. I never ate it. There was a fish and chip shop at the seven steps on Guinness Buildings (now buried) *it was a Jewish Fish and Chip shop and we went there in preference to Daltry's* (fried fish shop until 1999) *further up because you could buy pickled cucumbers there."*

I asked the people I interviewed who remembered this era about the levels of poverty on the Estate. Albert Lewis told me that in the late twenties and early thirties there were a few people "on their uppers" but that mostly people had enough food and a little spare cash to go to the Pictures or visit the pub. Sometimes even those whom you would have thought would have found life difficult managed to survive like Jack Longcroft, Ethel Zebedee's lodger who was deaf and dumb. Jack was a first class wood-carver and people would come from miles to get him to carve for them. This level of comfort was born out by the other interviewees. In general the picture emerges of a relatively poor but content society which was self sufficient in many ways. If you wanted furniture, someone made it for you. There were dairies which had cows for your milk. Particularly remembered was the metal cow at the back of the dairy on Columbia Road which had a metal dispenser with a spout. You put a penny in a slot and a measure of milk was delivered into your cup. There were bakeries like the one photographed in 1910 (p. 21) on the corner of Barnet Grove and Quilter Street and another on the corner of Baxedale Road and Barnet Grove which was there up until the second World War. If you could afford it local dressmakers made

right: *Oven still present in the basement of 65 Barnet Grove;* opposite: *Columbia Road during the week*

BARNET GROVE E.2

*Thomas Mitchell in his garden
in Durant Street, 1950s*

your clothes and if you couldn't second hand clothes were available from Kelly's on the corner of Barnet Grove and Wimbolt Street. Shops tended to stay open much later than they do today. George Renshaw reports on a Mr Manzi who lived in Elwin Street during the 1920s -1930s who supplied blocks of ice to the butchers before refrigeration was as widespread as today. In the summer Mr Manzi, known as old Jack, had an ice cream stall but in the winter he had a brazier from which he sold baked potatoes and chestnuts. Coffee stalls in the area would stay open all day and all night selling meat pies, savaloys, cheesecake and hot drinks. The butchers on the corner of Barnet Grove and Columbia Road too stayed open to feed the post pub crowds with boiled sheep's head and other local delicacies.

The major event during this period was war. Many people, as Ethel has already indicated, lost men folk in the first World War. My own family lost many including my grandfather who was killed in 1918 just before the signing of the armistice. Women, like my grandmother Alice who lived in Baxendale Street, were left without anyone to support them. Life was hard until their children left school and went to work themselves. These women supplemented any money they already earned by cleaning and taking in washing. The period from 1918 until well into the 1920s was tough for families without a male head.

Some men who were injured survived like Joyce Richardson's father Thomas Mitchell who came back to Durant Street. He became one of the first drivers on the Grey Green Coach line and had the distinction in 1928 of being booked for speeding at the spectacular speed of 27 miles 1365 yards per hour whilst on a trip to Horsham!

The Depression of the 1930s bit hard as unskilled work became scarce. Out of a UK population of fifty eight million, three million were out of work at its height. Technically though, the East End did not become a depressed area. While unemployment reached 66% in Jarrow, it never rose above 15% in Tower Hamlets. Of course, it depended on who you were and what you did.

Joyce Richardson in the park which replaced the bomb site on Durant Street

George Renshaw was born in Baxendale Street in 1922. He is a local historian and I am taking the description of how people managed to survive during that period from his monograph "Reflection of Changing Times".

"*My dad had been wounded three times during the 1914 Great War, he had also been gassed as well and through the depression times were very hard, nevertheless when work was available he would turn his hand to anything, and everything, as did most other people. My mum would go out in the early hours to do office cleaning and then do more cleaning at Wasems bakery in the Hackney Road. She would bring home day old cakes and stale bread that would be made into bread pudding. Markets in those days would stay open until 10 o'clock at night, the shops did not have any refrigeration and when it was getting late on Saturday night they would sell of any goods that would not keep. My mum would buy pig chitlings, cow heel and tripe and often we would have a lump of salt flank of beef with plenty of fat on it. She always bought the cheapest cut of meat.*

A friend of mine Billy Houghton would go with me to Spitalfields Market in Bishopsgate where we would collect the wooden boxes that had contained fruits and vegetables and drag them back home on a piece of rope. We would then chop them up and bundle them into firewood taking them around the streets and selling them for a halfpenny a bundle."

Even though times were hard George's story gives a rich evocation of community. A place where you really did leave your key on a string inside the letterbox and where you could trust your neighbours with your life.

The depression eased and the final few years of the 1930s were more affluent for most people.

Around the corner was another war, one which would change the face of East London forever.

George and Doreen Renshaw

the — SECOND

WORLD WAR

Reams, probably acres, of paper has been dedicated to recording the role which the civilian population of this area played in the Second World War (WW2). The East Ender's ability to survive is deservedly legendary. Particularly when you realise that the rich/poor divide was never more acute than when it came to sheltering from the bombs. Up West, bigger, better shelters and a willingness to allow the population to use deep underground shafts was the norm. In the East shelters were built by inexperienced Boy Scouts and the provision of shelters, such as they were, happened at a far slower rate than elsewhere. It is also true to say that the independent streak which had been exhibited when dealing with Lady Burdett Coutts was still firmly in place and, often, people sheltered exactly where they liked. A favourite place being underneath the railway arches in the vicinity of the Salmon and Ball Pub in Bethnal Green Road.

Despite the tube disaster of March 3, 1943 in which panic from a supposed air-raid resulted in 173 people being crushed to death, Bethnal Green Tube Station remained the safest place in the Borough. This had a sheltering capacity of 10,000 people and it played a great part in many peoples lives in times of danger. It was provided with a canteen, a sick bay with a nurse and a visiting doctor, a concert hall capable of holding 300 people and a complete branch public library consisting of 4,000 volumes.

As Ethel Zebedee reported the distribution of gas masks took place in September 1938 but it was not until the early hours of Sunday August 25 1940 that the war became a reality when several bombs weighing 50 kilograms each were dropped on Bethnal Green. The nearest to the Estate was that which landed on the Queen Elizabeth's Children's Hospital a mere fifty yards away.

The blitzkrieg began in earnest on September 7 when the Docks were set alight. The raids then continued without

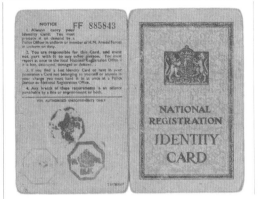

Identity card issued during World War 2

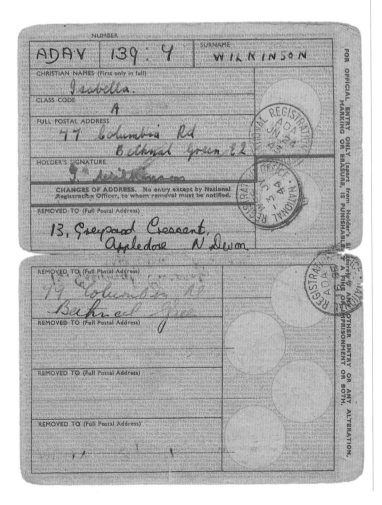

Local bomb damage in 1941. The clock tower of Columbia Market is visible above the debris opposite, centre right

a break until September 24. During that period 95 high explosive bombs ranging from 50-1,000 kilograms, two parachute mines and literally thousands of incendiary bombs fell on Bethnal Green. No part of the Borough was spared.

On the borders of the Estate a million to one chance saw a 50 kilogram bomb enter an air vent in Burdett Coutts Columbia Market which contained a very large public shelter causing many casualties.

Many men had already enlisted. Others like most of the men in my family were in essential industries, in their case producing the gas which was the universal way of cooking and heating in those days.

As the war accelerated and it was obvious that it was going to be a long haul more and more men felt impelled to enlist. Life was accelerated in more ways than one.

A few years earlier, in 1936, Ethel Zebedee and a friend had been hurrying along the street to the Pictures when she met the men who would become her two husbands;

"WE WERE RUNNING BECAUSE WE WERE A BIT LATE, WE'D ALMOST MISSED THE LAST HOUSE. I WAS FIFTEEN ALMOST SIXTEEN. WE RAN INTO THESE CHAPS AND I WENT FLYING. THE CHAP WHO PICKED ME UP SAID "I KNOW YOU." I DIDN'T KNOW HIM, BUT HE SAID HIS DAD WAS AT ONE POINT GOING TO GO WITH MY AUNT. ANYHOW THEY ASKED US WHERE WE WERE GOING AND WE TOLD THEM AND THEY SAID THEY WERE GOING TOO. WE WENT INTO THE 4D SEATS. THEY WANTED TO TREAT US BUT WE PAID OUR OWN WAY. THEY DIDN'T LIKE GOING UP IN THE GODS. AFTER THAT WE ALL WENT OUT TOGETHER SOMETIMES THEY'D LOSE THEIR FRIEND SYD CAUSE HE WAS THREE YEARS YOUNGER THAN THEM. SYD'S STILL AROUND AND LOOKS AFTER ME NOW. I WENT OUT WITH THE TWO BOYS UNTIL I WAS NEARLY EIGHTEEN. THE ONE I MARRIED THE SECOND TIME, LEN, SAID,

"WE CAN'T KEEP GOING ON LIKE THIS IT'S RIDICU-LOUS. THERE'S A WAR COMING, YOU OUGHT TO DECIDE WHICH ONE OF US YOU WANT." I WAS REALLY UNCOUTH AND I SAID "DO YOU MIND IF I PAL UP WITH GEORGE." LEN'S SISTER, WHO I STILL SEE, SAID HE CAME HOME AND BROKE HIS HEART.

ANY RATE WE GOT MARRIED THEN GEORGE ENLISTED WITHOUT TELLING ME BEFOREHAND. HE SAID HE COULDN'T STAND ALL HIS MATES FIGHTING FOR THE COUNTRY AND NOT HIM. CHARLIE MEISSEN WHO TALKED GEORGE INTO IT GOT FAILED ON HEALTH GROUNDS!"

ETHEL ZEBEDEE

Men who had never been further than Southend on Sea in Essex found themselves in aircraft or on ships crossing the Atlantic.

For the women left behind it was a tough life. Rationing hit the working classes particularly badly. People continued to help one another. Notable among these was Jack Garcia who owned the grocers shop at 150 Columbia Road. This part of the story is truly anecdotal but I was told that he bought on the black market and supplied many people with food with the proviso that they paid him after the war. Belts tightened, Germany looked set to be victorious and the bombing went on.

The two most notable hits on the Estate itself were on Guinness Buildings and Ion Square.

Marie Stephens grew up in Guinness Buildings here is her recollection of that raid and with it a snapshot of what life was like in the flats.

Outside Jack Garcia's shop at
150 Columbia Road 1950s

"When the bomb dropped in the playground of Guinness Buildings it made a huge crater which became filled with water. It blew down the Baxendale Arms Pub and two girls who lived opposite got killed. It also blew down those few houses in Baxendale Street (Nos 1-15) and the small shops and a couple of little houses at that end of Columbia Road. There were shops too at the corner of Shipton Street and Columbia Road. Bill the Barbers, Collins's powder, socks, lipstick that kind of thing, Leech's sweet shop, next to that was a glass and mirror shop. Then an entrance where someone kept a wheelbarrow most likely connected to the glass shop.

The brick built flats on Shipton Street (red brick) were built after the war. Before then they were little cottages which were very Victorian, the front door opened straight into the parlour. One man who lived in the cottages was a sweep and he had the sign outside. The cottages all went when the Baxendale went, it was a massive bomb.

It destroyed the baths. In Guinness Buildings we didn't have bathrooms but we had a bath block which is where the backs of the new flats in Baxendale Street now are. There were six blocks of flats A,B,C, D,E and F. I lived in D. The bath block had six or eight baths. The porters wife attended ladies day and girls night, men were on Sunday mornings. The baths were only for the residents of Guinness Buildings. The excess hot water was on tap the people who lived near (ABC) had huge enamel jugs and would go out and get the water."

The blast from that explosion also destroyed some of the roofs and the backs of the houses in Barnet Grove. If you look along the backs now you can see that houses 104-96 have had a considerable amount of brickwork replaced.

Ion Square was bombed on two separate occasions in November 1940 and March 1941 the second time with devastating results. Situated at the northern end of Durant Street, Ion Square had been built in 1845 and consisted of 38 small terraced cottages set out on three sides surrounding a small central garden.

The square had been provided with blast-shelters, the type designed for you to stand inside rather than a place to spend the night, however, many people were sheltering there. Also, so my mother told me, there were corrugated iron Anderson Shelters in the square.

Ernie Walkerdine was sheltering in his Anderson shelter in his garden in 22 Durant Street with his wife and two sons. It was two or three in the morning when he heard a whoosh followed by a bang. He recalls that the explosion hadn't seemed too bad but he was later told that

opposite: *The Queen Mother visiting allotments made upon cleared bomb sites, Shipton Street, 1943;*
right: *clearing bomb sites, 1941*

was because he was in the vortex of the explosion.

People had found a variety of places to shelter and my own extended family were sheltering from the bombs in the very shallow basement of the Royal Oak Pub on Columbia Road. My father, apparently, was happy with the thought of being drowned in beer from the huge barrels which the cellar contained, my mother was not so keen. Luckily they did not use the shelters in Ion Square which were situated a stones throw from their own houses in Baxendale Street.

My mother told me later that the land-mine had blown out nearly every window on the Estate and that from her perspective the blast had been enormous. Eventually the all clear sounded and people came to see what could be done.

Ion Square was a scene of carnage and death. Of the 38 houses only five were standing. Numbers 29-35 Durant Street were gone as were 35-47 Baxendale. It took until midday the following day before people buried in the houses were found.

left: *Bomb damage to the Columbia Market complex 1940;* below: *Bethnal green Road at the junction with Brick Lane looking west showing bomb damage 1941*

"IT WAS LIKE NIGHT GONE TO DAY.

Blood red the sky was with the flames.

BITS OF PEOPLE I KNEW LAY SCATTERED AROUND,

AN ARM HERE A LEG THERE,

even a head

AND IN THE MIDDLE OF IT THE AIR-RAID WARDEN.

we were all paralysed with shock, so was he.

I'LL NEVER FORGET HE LEANT DOWN,

PICKED UP AN ARM AND SHOOK IT OVER HIS HEAD,

BLOOD AND ALL RUNNING DOWN HIS FACE.

'FORGET THE DEAD,'

HE SCREAMED OUT.

'FOR CHRIST'S SAKE HELP ME
WITH THE LIVING.'

And we did."

I W

People have different recollections as to how many people died that night. Ernie Walkerdine estimates 17, Joyce Richardson 24. Other people recall loosing many school friends in the blast. People with relatives serving abroad mostly recollect the loss of one very important person.

"IN THE ION SQUARE BOMBING WE LOST OUR POSTMAN AND THAT BROKE OUR HEARTS MORE THAN ANYTHING. WE ALWAYS HAD THE SAME POSTMAN AND HE KNEW EVERYONE AND IF YOU GOT A LETTER FROM ABROAD AND ALL IT HAD ON IT WAS YOUR NAME HE KNEW IT WAS YOURS." EZ

Ethel is not being callous here, with your own streets being bombed and your loved ones fighting abroad facing goodness knows what, or your children evacuated far away, that link was so very important.

People tried to live as normally as they could and one of the most amazing thing in connection with the raids was the way people got into the habit of "clearing-up". Almost within seconds of a bomb exploding, people on the edges of the severe damage were seen with their brooms and brushes and dusters creating some sort of order out of the chaos. A sequel to every incident were neat piles of debris in the gutter in wait for the Council workers to take away.

A down side was looting. Ernie Walkerdine talks of this noting in particular that one of the people who had died in the Ion Square bombing had hidden her money inside a piano. Somehow a looter go to it before any of the poor woman's family or friends.

It was no longer an area of trust as dispossessed outsiders, and the frankly criminal, moved into the area.

Another stress on the populace was Evacuation. This had always been a mixed blessing with some good and bad experiences. Similarly with the women who joined the Land Army, some of whom couldn't wait to return home whilst others stayed where they were sent and built new lives for themselves.

In 1940 Gladys Herd and other children from the area were gathered in Columbia Road School before being evacuated.

Born in 1932 in nearby Cadell Street, Gladys was from a family of French Polishers who worked in the area. When she moved into Columbia Road she thought she had gone to heaven.

"WHEN WE FIRST MOVED AROUND COLUMBIA ROAD IN 1940 IT WAS THE FIRST ELECTRIC LIGHT WE EVER HAD. WE EVEN HAD A GEYSER FOR HOT WATER. IT WAS LOVELY, REALLY LOVELY, THEN THE WAR CAME."

Gladys with a group of other children was sent to the Yarmouth area and assembled in yet another hall. She was to be one of the lucky ones. A self-confessed child of little couth she was small and waifish. This is her story of what happened.

"WHEN WE GOT TO THE HALL IN YARMOUTH NOBODY WANTED US.

WE MUST HAVE LOOKED A ROUGH LOT MIND. I FINALLY GOT TAKEN IN BY A LOVELY FAMILY BUT THAT WAS STRANGE IN ITSELF BECAUSE THEY WEREN'T GOING TO HAVE ANY EVACUEES. THEIR DAUGHTER WAS A DWARF AND REALLY NOT WELL, SHE WAS 21 AT THE TIME. I FOUND OUT LATER THAT WHEN THE WIFE HEARD THAT THE CHILDREN IN THE HALL WERE BEING LEFT BEHIND SHE SAID TO HER HUSBAND, *"Willie I want you to go down and I want you to pick a little girl with no brothers and sisters and we'll have her."* ANY RATE HE PICKED ME. I'LL NEVER FORGET IT, HIM AND HIS BROTHER WALKED ME DOWN THE ROAD HOLDING MY HANDS ON EITHER SIDE. ALL I HAD WAS ON MY BACK, IT WAS A PILLOW CASE.

MY MUM HAD PUT ALL MY CLOTHES IN A PILLOW CASE BECAUSE I WAS TOO LITTLE TO CARRY A CASE. FINALLY WE GOT TO THEIR HOUSE, IT REALLY WAS A LOVELY COTTAGE. I WALKED IN AND ON THE STAIRCASE SHE HAD TERYLENE CURTAINS ALL DRAPED, IT WAS BEAUTIFUL.

GOODNESS KNOWS WHAT THEY THOUGHT BECAUSE I SAID IN MY WIDE ACCENT, *"Oh ain't it lovely it's just like what you see on the pictures."*

They had a maid. Every single breakfast time, lunch and evening meal the dining room table was laid with solid silver.

Can you imagine me going to that from around here? I was there for ten months and they accepted my family when they used to come and see me. They accepted my five brothers when they came home on leave and came up to visit me. They made them ever so welcome. I was supposed to be sent to Staffordshire as Yarmouth being near the sea wasn't thought to be safe. So my mother said 'I'll have her home.'

In the meantime the bombing in the East End was bad. They got in touch with my mother again and said that the bombing in Norfolk was nothing like as bad as it was in London and I went back. This time I kept crying as I wanted to go home. After two months my mother had me home.

I was fortunate, (unlike some of the others who were evacuated). They would have liked me to go and lived with them but I had family and I had to come home even though there was bombing."

Gladys kept in touch with that family right up until 1992 when the daughter finally passed away aged 82.

Ivy Chapman had a different story to tell. Born in 1919 she came to live in Baxendale Street just after the war having been bombed out of Stepney. In the interim she and her family found a place to stay in Kent.

"A friend of ours owned two cottages (hop picking huts) and he suggested going there. When we arrived this friend took us to the farmer who showed us the huts. It was early and hop picking hadn't started yet. There was me and my mum, my mum's friend and her three grown up children, so he gave us 4 huts as it was all empty. He said "When the hop picking starts I want you to answer 'yes' when I call for workers, because I want you all working for me."

We said yes, anything to get there to get a roof over our heads."

The backbreaking work and poor living conditions didn't suit them and finally Ivy and family decamped back to London to face the bombs again.

Others would not leave like Marie Stephens who told her mother. 'If I'm made to go I'm coming back and bringing the boys (my brothers) back with me.'

Marie still corresponds with women who lived in Guinness Buildings during the war some of whom became GI brides and have lived in America ever since.

Ivy Chapman

She also kept in touch with another woman as she recalls:

"I HAD A FRIEND WHO WENT INTO THE LAND ARMY AND MARRIED A MAN IN WARWICKSHIRE. WHEN I VISITED HER IN LYMINGTON SPA I USED TO HAVE TO TAKE HER PIES WITH THE LIQUOR IN A STERILISED MILK BOTTLE WITH A FLIP TOP. MASH SHE COULD DO HERSELF BUT NOT THE REST. SHE WAS HOMESICK FOR BETHNAL GREEN HER WHOLE LIFE. THERE'S NOTHING WORSE THAN CHRONIC HOMESICKNESS."

The war ended and as you can see from the photographs the Estate celebrated in style. In the centre of the photograph on pages 78-79, posing like mad is Diamond Lil who never joined the land army, or any army for that matter, because she was a he and is part of the folklore of the Estate.

More of Lil later.

The surviving men returned, Labour was elected into power and the Estate took stock of the last six years. Bethnal Green had seen 550 people killed, 400 seriously injured and 5,583 homes either destroyed or seriously damaged. Given how bad it might have been for an area sandwiched between the Docks and the City it had escaped quite lightly.

NEVERTHELESS THE ESTATE WAS ABOUT TO ENTER A LONG PERIOD OF DECLINE AND CHANGE. IT HAD SURVIVED THE WAR ALMOST INTACT BUT OTHER FORCES WOULD THREATEN ITS EXISTENCE MORE RADICALLY THAN ANY BOMB. THE DESIRE FOR CHANGE, OF EXCHANGING NEW FOR OLD, WAS IN THE AIR. HIGH RISE FLATS BEGAN TO SPROUT LIKE CONCRETE CARBUNCLES AND THE HEART OF EAST LONDON BEGAN TO BLEED AWAY TO THE SUBURBS, PRINCIPALLY THOSE OF ESSEX.

1950 ———— 1970

DECLINE & FALL

THE POST WAR CLEARING UP AND REBUILDING OF THE ESTATE TOOK A VERY LONG TIME. THE BOMBED ENDS OF BAXENDALE STREET WERE CLEARED AND GARAGES ERECTED. HOUSES WHICH WERE AFFECTED BY BLASTS WERE PART REBUILT AND WINDOWS AND ROOFS REPLACED THE JESUS HOSPITAL CHARITY, WHO WERE STILL IN CONTROL OF THE ESTATE, FOUND THE DRAIN ON THEIR MONEY WHICH THIS RENOVATION CAUSED PARTICULARLY IRKSOME.

On the streets themselves men returned from war and life began to take on some semblance of normality. Many of the shopkeepers had fled during the War and although many old faces remained, it was obvious that the area was changing.

As children we played on bomb sites, which were the only source of open land in those days.

The first one of these playgrounds to disappear was the Black Buildings, Baroness Burdett Coutts stately pile which was demolished in 1957. As children we had delighted in playing it what remained of this sepulchral space. The whole of the complex and Hassard Street was razed. On the Estate itself repairs carried on at a leisurely rate. Streets were still blissfully

opposite: Shot across the back of Columbia Road (now demolished) 1952; above: Demolition of Columbia Market 1957

free of traffic and children played on them secure in the knowledge that we were safe.

Being born in 1952, I particularly remember this time. Although I lived on the wrong side of Columbia Road at number 77, I was as much part of the Estate as anyone else. Our houses, built far later than the Estate, had been constructed for the occupation of wood-workers for the back yard of the houses led into the workshops of Ezra Street courtyard. Before the war the houses and yard had been one but now they were split. I grew up with the constant noise of buzz saws and the ever present wood chippings which, before regulation, drifted thickly through the air.

Life, really wasn't very different to that which Ethel, Albert and the others have described. We still shopped mostly on Columbia Road which had its butchers, bakers and boot menders. There were more cars on the street and soon television would become a constant companion.

One thing which hadn't changed for most of us was the state of our houses. The majority still had no heating, cold water only and an outside toilet. The houses were very damp, it was if the watercress beds wanted to reclaim their own. Fungus sprouted on the interior walls and people, expectant of a new post-war life, began to look elsewhere for accommodation.

For the first time ever protectioneering reared its ugly head. Shop windows were broken and men of stocky build and no brain threatened Armageddon if people didn't pay up.

People, like Jack Garcia and my Aunts, did not pay up and not much happened as they has little stock and little to lose and the heavy men moved on elsewhere.

Former button factory
Hackney Road, 1982

Pollution was thick in the air as post war we burnt tar blocks to keep warm and rationing kept us hungry. It was not all gloom, doom and despondency though we had our share of excitement and our share of characters. Every area has them, the people who stand out whether by dint of eccentricity or sheer bloody mindedness.

The person I am about to describe had a huge impact on my life and, I suspect, on many other people's. In the late fifties I would sit on the step of my home and stare across at the Newspaper shop and wait. The sun would be glinting onto her jewellery long before I saw her. Poodle tucked under arm, cigarette smoke curling at the end of a fine holder, high heeled slippers bulging with artificial fur, along the street came Diamond Lil. It was many years before I realised that she was a he for nobody ever mentioned otherwise.

Recently I read and watched the paroxysms which the House of Lords went through on dealing with homosexuality and I thought of Lil.

Lil was a long term acquaintance of my maternal grandmother, Isabella (the fifth in a long line). Pieces of Lil's story have been given to me by most of the interviewees.

Joyce Richardson remembers the first time Lil had her hair peroxided. Marie Stephens who grew up with Lil in Guinness Buildings went on the hunt for information for me and found out the following.

"Given name Harry Young he was born and lived in the Broadway Market area (E8) and in later years in Guinness Buildings. Lil always worked manually in local shops; like the pie shop on Hackney Road. Lil had three or four brothers who gave her a hard time. She had a doting mother with whom she lived. Diamond was a very caring person; not a bad word was ever heard about her. Lil's "friend" was Maisie (given name not known) surname Townsend. Maisie and Lil were always quarrelling in public. Unlike Lil, Maisie was quite a grotesque figure with her own over the top makeup and dark nail polish. Maisie was also from the Broadway."

My grandmother too was from the Broadway. If you look at the only photograph we have of Lil on the right is a small, wide woman with whom Lil is linking arms. That is my grandmother and she and Lil used to sing in the pubs around here. Lil sang in The Perseverance on Barnet Grove but was a regular at the Royal Oak.

Gladys Herd recalls Lil and Maisie seated at opposite ends of the bar in post row snarling mode. They were the archetypal drag queens, bitchy, quick with a reposte but above all glamorous in a time when the world was particularly grey. In later life Lil cleaned the toilets in the Nag's Head Pub on Hackney Road. As Joyce Richardson recalled,

"She hated cleaning the men's loos, she thought it was demeaning. Lil was a woman you see."

below: *Linda Wilkinson and Marie Stephens. Barnet Grove, Summer 1955*
following pages: *The jolly boys outing from the Royal Oak late 1950s*

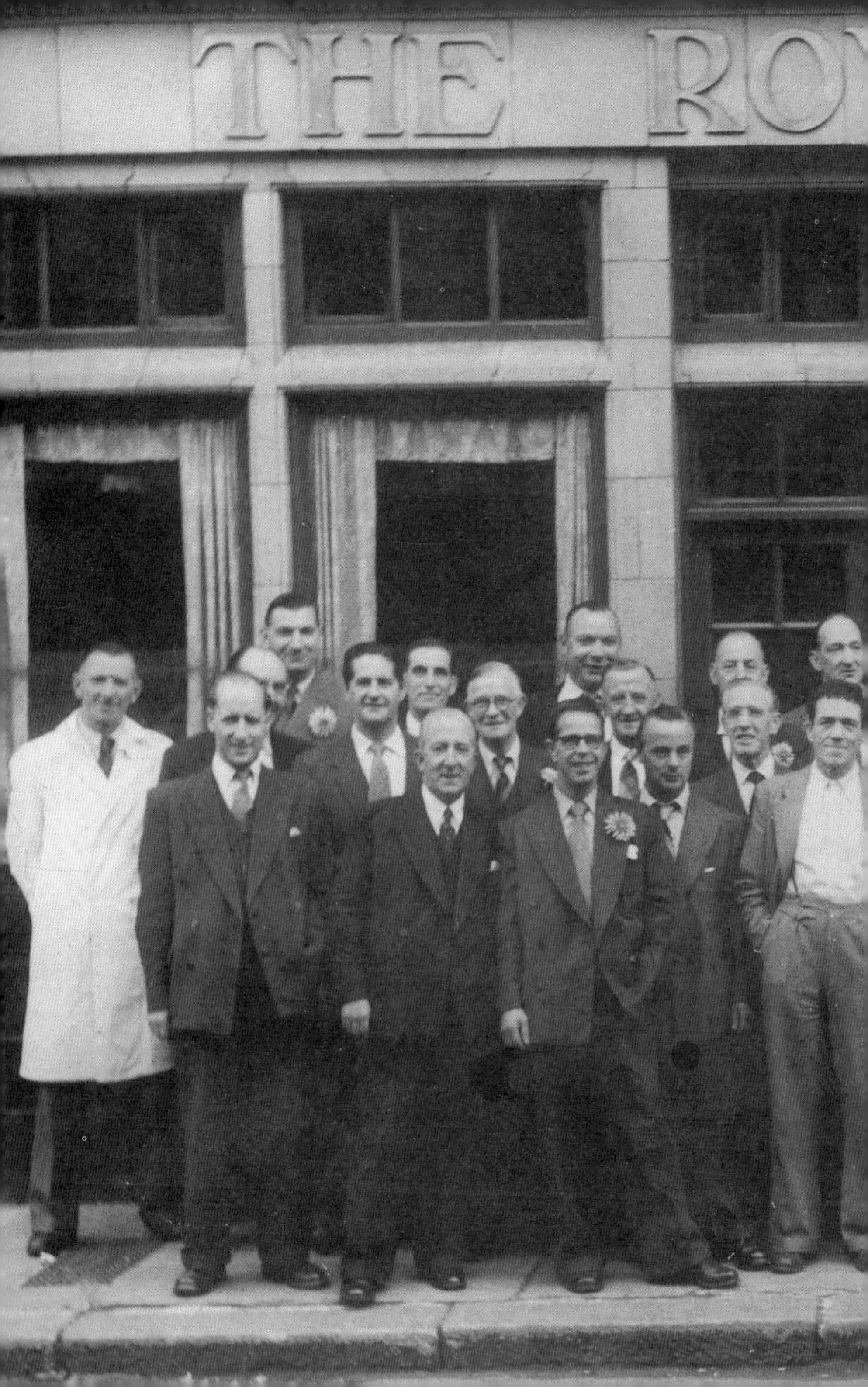
THE RO

Columbia Road cricket team triumphant at Lords 30 September, 1965

If only such tolerance of all differences was more widespread.

The last time I saw Lil was in 1970 when I delivered post to Guinness Buildings in the Christmas Holidays. She had me in for a cup of tea and I was astounded to see an altar with candles and a large picture of Maisie who had died not so long before.

Lil's teeth and fingertips were brown with nicotine but her head was a riot of carefully coiffed white. She was obviously lost without Maisie.

"*I miss that little bugger,*" Lil said dragging on yet another one of the cigarettes which would hurry her to her grave. "*Funny, never thought I would.*"

I was at a loss for words so I drank my tea and left; I never saw Lil again.

Other less savoury characters blossomed in the area. Late on one night in the sixties we were woken by a screech of brakes and the sounds of sirens. As always thinking the war was back people fled onto the street. One of the girls who lived along by us had married a chap who had become involved in a large robbery. Somehow he had escaped from jail and headed home to see her. Finding her, not to be alone, shall we say he proceeded to lose his rag in a big way. Someone must have called the police who were very pleased to re-arrest him and cart him back to jail.

Another night we heard a similar screech of brakes followed by a crash. Out on Columbia Road we saw a car rammed against a lamppost and three men running away from it. My mother didn't notice the car but joined the men in running to help in what she surmised was an accident.

Moments later, pale and shaking, she returned home. One of the men had pointed a gun at her and told her not too politely to *"Piss off if you don't want to get shot."*

Doreen Renshaw has a more uplifting tale from the times. Lords cricket ground, for the first time ever, invited Schoolchildren in to play on that hallowed space. The shot of the team from Columbia Road Primary School in 1965 says it all really. We are not an area known for cricketers but the school coach did his damndest and, against all odds, the team won.

Columbia Road as a shopping street was slowly dying. Tesco's on Bethnal Green Road first opened it's doors in the early 1960s and the small shopkeepers on the Estate either aged and were unable to maintain their shops or left due to competition.

Although the Flower Market was still in existence it was then a small, local, affair and GRADUALLY THE SHOPS BECAME EMPTY AND MANY WERE BOARDED UP.

On the main Estate houses were also standing empty and semi-derelict, as people either died or moved away. The houses, although still cheap, were unrentable.

Mrs Stephens with two of her grandchildren and Harry Wilkinson, Columbia Road 1970s

pages 90-91: *Celebrating King George V's silver jubilee, 1935. Mrs King is second from left standing top right, page 91*
pages 92-93: *Quilter Street decorated for VE Day, 1945*
opposite and above: *The coronation celebrations on Quilter Street and Coronation commemorative card;*

A

CHANGING

WORLD

Some three hundred years after the pastureland in Stebonheath was acquired to become the Jesus Hospital Estate and some one hundred and twenty years (or so) after the houses were built it was time to bow to changing times.

Unable to satisfy the demands of the various statutory bodies within Tower Hamlets (LBTH) to renovate the houses the Charity sought to dispose of its property in East London.

In 1960 the area was considered by the LBTH for clearance and demolition to make way for open space and roads. The twentieth century Visitors from the Charity were far from impressed by this proposal feeling that the houses were in good order.

The houses were not in good order however. Many still lacked hot water and an inside toilet. Repairs, when performed, were rudimentary and the writing looked to be on the wall. As Carolyn Clarke who moved into the area in 1979 recalls two of the houses on the Estate were still lit entirely by gas and had never been connected to the electric mains. In spite of this the locals felt that the Charity had not been bad landlords and they mounted a spirited defence of the area. I remember my parents attending meetings at the town hall and there was talk of barricading the streets.

In the end it was discovered that neither the Greater London Council (GLC) nor the LBTH had the jurisdiction to clear the area. However, not daunted, in

1971 an application was made by the GLC for a Compulsory Purchase order which would designate five areas of the Estate as clearance areas resulting in the demolition of 190 houses. Once more the Visitors, although they not feel they could continue to maintain the Estate, fought to keep it intact. Accordingly a Public Enquiry into the matter was held at Bethnal Green Town Hall in October 1972.

Like an echo from the early days, the gentlemen from the Charity continued their run of bad luck for their managing agent had a heart attack in the middle of giving evidence and had to be rushed to Bethnal Green Hospital from whence he issued written notes to be read out at the hearing.

Their endeavours were not in vain however, because only one area was designated for clearance, that area now known as Jesus Green. This was set aside for the erection of a crèche but subsequent discovery of subsidence in the centre lead to it being left at the much loved green we have today.

The proposed destruction of these houses caused much consternation at the time as the photograph shows. Although the houses around this triangle overlooked a wood yard and small industrial units people did not wish to move. It seemed

Waiting for demolition, Quilter Street, 1971

to them that the houses were in no worse a condition than many others. In 1975 under the fair rents scheme, the Charity were able to effect the part modernisation on numbers 66-96 Quilter Street, but they could neither sustain the expense, nor the speed which LBTH required them to complete renovations.

At this point in time the houses were rented out at £3 per week, far lower than other properties in the area.

The battle to save the Estate from either destruction or gentrification continued. The fear was that if the area survived that it would simply become an adjunct to the City, providing second homes for businessmen who did not wish to commute during the week but who would flee to the countryside during the weekend. Newspaper reports abounded and with them, added confusion as to the age of the Estate. In 1979 the Hackney Gazette proclaimed the houses on the Estate to be 150 years old, this would have them being built in 1829. In 1979 the residents of the Estate founded the Jesus Hospital Estate Residents Association (JHERA) in order to *"fight the slow death of the traditional community."*

below: Prince of Wales marriage celebrations 1981;
right: JHERA summer fete mid 1980s.

Alf Dear from the Association is reported in the press as saying. "*Most tenants have no inside toilets, baths or hot water and one house still has only gas lighting.*" The fight to persuade the Charity to keep the houses was lost. Their final act was to negotiate for the tenants the right to buy the freehold of their houses at a discounted rate. Some did, many didn't and the houses passed firstly through the hands of Wanderslaw Ltd, who purchased the houses for £4,000 each before trying to sell them on to the residents for £20,000 each.

The Association fought this unrealistic and greedy manoeuvre and finally barted the price down to £8,000 each. However, once on the open market the houses were snapped up. When Carolyn moved into the area she recalls many of the houses as being empty. The first freehold sold to a non-resident was in 1979 which was £15,000 two weeks later the next went for £20,000.

The Association though was going from strength to strength. With the aid of a grant from the Housing Action (working was under the auspices of the GLC) the Association was able to facilitate the modernisation of St Peters' Church Hall in which they met.

The first fete on the newly formed Jesus Green was in 1981 and it was a huge success. As Carolyn recalls:

"The beauty of it was

EVERYONE ON THE ESTATE KNEW EACH OTHER

AND WHAT EACH OTHER DID FOR A LIVING.

SO IF YOU NEEDED A LORRY TO CARRY GEAR

OR EVEN A ROPE FOR A TUG OF WAR

SOMEONE GOT IT

(THE LATTER FROM TRUMAN'S BREWERY IN BRICK LANE).

THINGS WERE SO EASY;

EVERYONE KNEW

A MAN WHO WOULD."

Carolyn Clarke

The Association had community arts workshop in Oxford House, there were Beanos to Brighton, Christmas dances, trips to France. In short the community which remained was as strong as it had ever been.

On the logistical front they fought off plans to change traffic flow which would have turned the Estate into a rat run, fought off the plans to extend a motorway through the middle of it, but things were changing.

Slowly and inexorably the mix of population shifted. At first the houses were cheap enough for people to buy them as second homes. More and more the area, as had been feared, became a ghost town at weekends. Something else occurred as Carolyn noted:

"We lost all our children. There were none to be seen. They make community as much as anything else and they weren't there."

For the old community who still rented their properties the world was not a better place. The rent collector for the new landlord was frequently mugged and tenants had to trek to North London to pay their rents. Wanderslaw was superseded by Bliss and then Napier Green and Company, acting on behalf of the current owners Pearl and Coutts.

For those tenants who did not purchase their houses the present weekly rent is £67 plus £7 rates. Although some improvements were made some people still live in houses with an outside toilet, no real heating and poorly installed electricity.

From an open market rate of £15,000 pounds in 1980; by 1984 the average sale price had reached £30,000; in 1986 this was £60,000 and this figure has risen inexorably through the highs and lows of the property market to sit in the year 2001 at an astounding £300,000 plus. Were the tenants right to fear, has the area turned into an extension of Surrey borders? Some people feel it has, some feel otherwise.

Corner of Baxendale Street and Barnet Grove

THE

old T
H
E new

AND THE

MARKET

2OO1

I HAD LIVED ABROAD AND ALSO, STRANGELY, IN BARNET IN NORTH LONDON. I HAD BEEN AWAY FROM THE ESTATE SINCE 1974 WHEN IN 1985 I CAME BACK WITH SOME FRIENDS WHO HAD HEARD ABOUT THIS "FABULOUS OLD MARKET IN THE EAST END."

I DIDN'T LET ON THAT I HAD COME FROM THE AREA. I EXPECTED TO SEE THE MARKET WHICH I HAD LEFT IN THE EARLY SEVENTIES WHICH WAS SMALL AND POPULATED BY LOCALS. WHEN I HAD LEFT INDOOR PLANTS WERE BECOMING POPULAR, NOW ON CHRISTMAS EVE 1985, I COULD HARDLY BELIEVE THE HUSTLE AND BUSTLE. POT SHOPS HAD TAKEN OVER THE DERELICT SHOPS ON COLUMBIA ROAD AND THE PLACE WAS BUZZING.

Linda Wilkinson outside her home

I sat in the Royal Oak over a drink and a lump rose in my throat. I knew why I had never come back, I knew what I would feel. My friends chatted on happily whilst I drifted into the past. On the way back to trendy Hampstead, where I was then living, we walked up Barnet Grove and I was astounded to see Jesus Green where the oil shop and houses had been. Over the next month I couldn't shake the feeling I'd had. In late January my partner and I bought a house in Barnet Grove and in May 1986 I finally came home.

I had become used to suburban ways and had reasoned that nobody would be left from the past, nobody would know me. It would be the adjunct to the suburbs as had been predicted. I had become attuned to different ways I suppose, in Barnet people had changed houses as frequently it seemed as they changed their socks.

The moving van drove off, the doorbell rang, I answered and there stood Ginger Lil. Now grey haired she had lived in a nearby house on Columbia Road when I was growing up.

Arms crossed under breasts she surveyed me acutely. *"Heard you was back. I told the others I'd welcome you home. Glad you're home Lin, hope you stay."*

I swallowed hard and replied that I was home for good.

"That's all right then," she said and walked off.

Over the years others too have come back like Marie Stephens who married her husband Derek in the 1960s. He was a coal miner from Shropshire and she went to live there. She had a lovely three bedroomed house and garden.

Marie Stephens on the site where the Baxendale Arms once stood

"I USED TO COME BACK TO BETHNAL GREEN EVERY MONTH. THIS ONE WEEKEND WHEN WE WENT BACK TO SHROPSHIRE, DEREK WAS GOING TO WORK NIGHT-SHIFT. HE WENT TO BED EARLY AND CAME DOWN FOR SOMETHING AND FOUND ME CRYING WITH HOMESICKNESS. THAT WAS IT, "I'M NOT HAVING THAT", HE SAID. I SAT CUDDLING A VACUUM FLASK FULL OF PEA SOUP WHICH MUM HAD MADE ME AND CRYING MY EYES OUT. IT WAS STUPID BUT I FELT REALLY LOST. I COULD NEVER PUT IT INTO WORDS, I STILL CAN'T.

I USED TO WALK AROUND THAT BEAUTIFUL COUNTRYSIDE IN SHROPSHIRE AS IF I WERE WALKING BESIDE MYSELF, IT WAS AWFUL. I GO BACK THREE OR FOUR TIMES A YEAR FOR A WEEK IT'S LOVELY, BUT FOR ME A WEEK IS ENOUGH."

I suppose we can be forgiven for being dyed in the wool locals so we'll pass on the nostalgia and look at some more recent emigrants to the area.

During the week Columbia Road is very quiet. Most of the shops are nowadays either dedicated to selling goods related to gardens, or only open on Sundays to catch the trade. There are a few stalwarts who keep the street going and who have now become part of the tapestry of the area.

154 Columbia Road has been a newsagents since the 1891 census. Ten years prior to that it had been a wet-fish shop, one assumes at the time Baroness Coutts was attempting to house Billingsgate Fish Market in that august building at the end of the road.

Yusuf Gulamali, know to everyone as Joe, is the latest in that long line of newsagents. His is one of only three Asian families on the Estate and came

to the street in 1988. He was born in Tanzania but is of Indian Gujarati decent. In 1977 Yusuf got a place to read Geology & Chemistry at Goldsmiths College, London. He experienced a lot of racism there and moved on within a year.

After several years in various forms of commerce he decided that he wanted his own business. As East London had a particularly bad name for racism he tried to avoid going there; but that was where all the opportunities were.

He recalls:

"The closeness to the City was attractive. And when I visited the shop on a Sunday I saw the flower market and was sold on the place. I liked the feel of the area. The owner before me was another Gujarat. He told me that there was no trouble in the area, but he was in fact leaving because of difficulties he was having with settling into the area and the racism he was encountering. I had a different approach to dealing with comments and didn't get angry and abusive with my customers. I was patient and made my position clear over time by passing subtle comments.

THE FIRST CHARACTER I REMEMBER WAS MRS KING IN ELWIN STREET. SHE SEEMED TO BE THE QUEEN OF THE AREA AND WAS TO BE RESPECTED. WHEN SHE WALKED INTO THE SHOP FOR THE FIRST TIME SHE ASKED ME IF I WAS THE NEW OWNER, WHAT MY NAME WAS AND THEN INTRODUCED HERSELF. I TOLD HER THAT I HOPED THAT SHE WOULD PATRONISE MY SHOP. SHE SAID. "YOU LOOK AFTER US, WE'LL LOOK AFTER YOU." FROM THAT DAY ONWARDS THINGS WERE EASIER, SHE HAD ENDORSED, MY SHOP AND ME IN THE COMMUNITY."

Yusuf (Joe)

Joe is proud to think he has done his bit for the area, coming in as an outsider. His shop is a focal point and he is accepted by the new comers and older established people. It's taken ten years to do this. Even as an Asian and an outsider and a newcomer he has established the only axis on the estate where all types of people intersect. Joe has an advisory role too as residents share problems and difficulties with him, which shows a trust and reliance.

Along the road at 148 is Columbia Video run by Steve. Once a professional footballer and self confessed jack of all trades Steve's father in law told him about the video shop being up for sale back in 1988.

Steve though is one of those who came back to the area. Born in Stepney he came to live in Wimbolt Street with his grandfather when he was one year old. After spells in South London and Margate he came back to the area some years ago.

Like Yusuf, his shop is often more of a social surgery than a simple rental service.

Although it was a video shop before, Steve found that the films he'd inherited were illegal copies, all two hundred of them and the newly replaced roof he had similarly inherited came off in the first high wind.

Life running a small, independent video rental business is not easy as Steve relates.

"Business was good enough for the first five or six years, but satellites hit it quite badly and I thought it would never pick up again, but after six months it did when people realised they weren't seeing new films on satellite any quicker than they could through me.

THIS IS A REAL COMMUNITY SHOP, IT'S NEVER GOING TO BE A BIG EARNER, NEVER, BUT I GET BY. PEOPLE GO TO OTHER SHOPS BUT THEY COME BACK. THEY TELL ME ALL THEIR TROUBLES. A LITTLE PSYCHOLOGIST I AM SOMETIMES, WHAT THEY TELL ME GOES NO FURTHER THAT THEY ALL KNOW.

Steve

I buy the videos from a wholesaler and they are good to me. I get most films on the day of release, some though are not financially worth my while. For instance the Green Mile cost me sixty pounds a copy but Blockbuster gets it for five pounds. They've got this share revenue scheme going with the companies, at the end of eight weeks they put them up for sale for twenty pounds, I can't fight that kind of competition. It's difficult at times to keep going. For instance I got four copies of Gladiator at forty five pounds a throw plus vat. A month later it came out to buy. How on earth are you going to make a living against those odds?

The companies are shortening the windows on the film releases more and more. Now there are a few films coming out to rent or buy on same day which isn't too bad for me as lot's of people don't want to buy.

When I first came here people wanted action and martial arts films, now I get more call for European and art house movies. I don't have hardly any karate films in the shop these days, they don't rent. The new people who move in around here seem to be doing well and the area has changed in so many ways.

When I look at these houses you couldn't give them away when I was a kid. If you moved in round here it was admitting you were at the bottom of the pile, really poor. Funny to think the whole place is built on watercress beds. There's no piling under these houses, just clay. Look at the fishing tackle shop up the road it

had to be repiled the whole building collapsed inwards.

There's quite a basic stable population around here now. Not many for sale notices are going up these days. As a community it sticks together, just wish they'd stick together more about the filming."

Filming is a sore point with many people. As much as some aren't bothered by street closures and stars milling around, Steve's business is frequently affected as much of the filming which does happen is in Columbia Road and access to his shop is often difficult and compensation not necessarily a given.

As we both agreed, it's strange to think for so long that nobody wanted to know the area but nowadays nobody can get enough.

Across the road in the Royal Oak Pub, Mervyn the landlord has a different take on filming. He has deliberately kept the inside as original as he can in order to promote his pub for use by film companies. The Royal Oak hasn't always had quite such a benign usage though.

Mervyn is originally from Edinburgh and came down when he lost his job back in the early eighties. He had various catering jobs but decided he wanted his own place. He'd moved to Canning Town, in the late eighties.

"I got offered a pub in Kingsland Road as

Mervyn and Sheba

a tenancy, but I had my car stolen and didn't much like that particular area. We were in a cab on the way to the cash and carry one day and I was talking away to my mate, saying the pubs are expensive etc.. The taxi driver turned around and said his brother-in-law was selling his pub the Royal Oak in Columbia Road. It cost us nothing to have a look so we came down the road one night and walked past it. It was an expensive lease and we thought he (the landlord) must be crazy for the asking price. We didn't go in that night but came back, opened the door Eugene, Kenny and myself and thought "Oh this is exactly what we were looking for." We got talking to the bloke and bartered him down. What we didn't know was that it was a drug pub, it was known to all and sundry as The Royal Coke.

I had a partner come in with me as I couldn't afford it by myself. We did a search as the Flower Market was then rumoured to be under threat of closure. Luckily that wasn't going to happen so we took The Oak.

My partner was straight and I'm gay. I could have made the pub gay only but I wanted to make it a mixed local. In the last nine years we've managed to build up a relationship with the local community but it took some doing. We used to get firebombed, kids broke our windows. For the first few years the market people were afraid to come in to drink because of HIV. But now they come in all the time. Now it's settled down we have a good community spirit; we do a lot of charity work for the Mildmay (a local HIV hospice) and other causes."

I asked Mervyn how he found the people having got to know the area.

'I find it very friendly. For example I was living in Canning Town for over eight years but I hardly spoke to my next door neighbour. I was broken into twice. Once you move here and have been around for a couple of years you are accepted and that's that. Everybody knows everybody on the street. People are so friendly and helpful it's so different from other parts of London.

I now realise that part of the violence we had in the early days was because we were turning it around into a community pub not a drug pub.

THE DAY WE TOOK OVER IT GOT RAIDED.

THEY (THE POLICE) CAME FLYING UP THE ROAD, SUDDENLY THE DOOR BURST OPEN AND ABOUT TWELVE DRUG SQUADDIES CAME IN.

We thought it was a joke for the guy who was leaving.

BUT WHEN I REALISED THAT THERE REALLY WAS A GUY LYING ON THE FLOOR WITH A GUN TO HIS HEAD I KNEW IT WAS FOR REAL. THEY JUMPED OVER THE BAR AND HANDCUFFED ME AND MY PARTNER. ONCE EVERYBODY WAS HANDCUFFED THEY SLAPPED DOWN A WARRANT TO SEARCH THE PLACE FOR DRUGS.

WE DISCOVERED THAT THE CITY GENTS WERE COMING IN BUYING HALF A PINT OF BEER FOR TWENTY FIVE QUID, TAKING THE DRUG THEY WERE PASSED WITH THEIR CHANGE, GOING INTO THE LOO DOING THEIR BUSINESS AND THEN LEAVING.

People still thought it was going to be gay only but the problem wasn't really about that I think it ran at a deeper level. It was like something else was being taken away, first it was drugs, then it was gay but it wasn't and now I hope it isn't like that I'd like it to be for everyone.'

Mervyn's pub has been used for filming many of the most notable movies and series to be seen in the recent past. The list includes The Krays, Lock Stock and Two Smoking Barrels and Goodnight Sweetheart. Recently Blue Peter did a shoot in the Oak which featured Pearly Kings and Queens but as Meryn rightly commented.

"I knew it was all wrong, the Pearlies are from South London, but it was fun and the Pearlies themselves didn't seem to mind."

Before Yusuf, Mervyn and Steve, Isabel had already set up shop. She came from Galicia in Northern Spain and took over number 93 Columbia Rd in 1981.

"I took over from Iris who had the place as a fruit and vegetable shop. It was nothing like now, I'm telling you, nothing. The shop, like all of the others, was completely run down. When we did it up we took so many bags of rubbish out.

There were sacks of potatoes stuck up the chimney upstairs. They were there for insulation to stop the cold I suppose, but there were enough of them to fill half a skip.

THERE WAS NO POTTERY STUFF ON COLUMBIA ROAD ONLY RUN DOWN SHOPS WHICH WERE REALLY FALLING TO PIECES I HAD A ROUGH TIME ON COLUMBIA ROAD, I'M GOING TO TELL YOU. I DIDN'T HAVE VERY MUCH ENGLISH THEN AND I WAS TREATED VERY BADLY. THE FRONT OF THE SHOP WAS SET ON FIRE, THAT WAS AROUND 1985.

I BEEN HAVE SHOT AT BY AIR GUNS WHICH WERE FIRED THROUGH THE WINDOW AND THROUGH THE OLIVE OIL BOTTLES. I HAD ABUSIVE PHONE CALLS, THE LOT. WHEN I LIVED IN SHOREDITCH I USED TO HAVE BULLETS THROUGH THE WINDOW TOO.

EVERYTHING STOPPED WHEN I GO TO KNOW TOM WHO USED TO RUN SECOND HAND SHOP ON THE CORNER; HE WAS A LOCAL YOU SEE.

Isabel

My cousin used to live upstairs and his wife used to be abused all the time in the street, we both were. It was people in and around from the flats, people we saw everyday who did it. People would walk into the shop, put their hands to their noses and say, "It stinks in here."

Soon the place began to change, in fact since I've been here I've seen this area change a minimum of three to four times. Now is the best it has ever been because there is a wonderful mix of people and nobody challenges anybody. Dealing with the public I can see it.

In the early day, when the area was so run down, there was a completely different set of people. After that came people who had children and then moved out of the area, after that things began to get a bit better but now it is a good mixture.

Maurice who I met, who used live over the road in those early days, had a lot of abuse because he was gay. That was 12-14 years ago and it was just not accepted.

There are still some people around who don't like foreigners or gays but there is always going to be someone like that, otherwise it's not part of life. You don't even look at these people you just ignore them.

The majority of the people here now are wonderful. People are staying more than before.

A lot of gay people are buying the properties, they don't have children and they don't move on. A lot of people with careers who work in the City live here and they don't move on like they did before. I notice now that the same people have been here three to four years, it never used to be like that.

I had the delicatessen for a while as a rental then I wanted to buy the property. The landlords wouldn't sell 93 without 95. I couldn't really afford it as the delicatessen wasn't paying that kind of money, but I bought them. We were living in a rented house and it seemed ridiculous having two shops and have nowhere to live. So we sold 95 to Carl from the market. The places were in a terrible state and he spent the same amount he paid again in doing it up. I bought a house where we lived for a while. I was working very hard in the delicatessen but it wasn't paying me back. By then I loved living here, the community was changing and I didn't want to be anywhere else. So I decided to open the Tapas bar and live here full time.

I will never sell 93 it was a gift to me. When I came here people used to say, "Why Columbia Road, you're crazy it's horrible", but now it's the place to be.

Even today though the shops on Columbia are not maintained at all there are holes through the roofs. It's disgraceful the way Pearl and Coutts have let them go, they charge enough for rent and they don't maintain them at all.

A lot of the older folk still can't accept the foreigners but things are changing. Mervyn in the Oak has done a great deal to change things, especially for gays. We're all people after all. Look at him he's a disabled man and he doesn't take anything from the government.

He works hard to survive, he doesn't make money he just gets by. People should look up to Mervyn. When he came and he put up the rainbow flag people wanted to put an article in the Evening Standard saying how awful it was and how he should take the flag down.

They asked me to support them, I went mental. People are so ignorant, it was young people too at the time, not old. I threw them out of my place.

THESE DAYS THOUGH EVERYONE SUPPORTS EACH OTHER AND WE ARE THERE FOR EACH OTHER.

I HAVE NEVER LIVED SO LONG ANYWHERE IN MY LIFE. I DON'T THINK I COULD LIVE ANYWHERE ELSE."

Of course the mix of attitudes about the way the area has altered is wide and diverse.

Many of the remaining older population feel that their lives are impoverished, that the community they grew up with has been replaced by people they cannot understand. The soaring house prices and middle class accents which surround them are as alien a territory as the most recent wave of immigrants, the Bangladeshis, seem to be. This latest Diaspora is a long way from integration into the wider community and racism is a sad, but present, reality.

Others see that without the influx of new house owners that the area would have been bulldozed. That the projected motorway extension from Victoria Park would have become a reality and that Jesus Green would be part of yet another juggernaut route.

Some older folk feel trapped in their houses, others have retained community. The patchwork of many hues, and attitudes, is as present now as it ever was.

above and opposite: *Interior*
Elwin Street

For six days a week Columbia Road during the day is almost somnolent. Lee's Seafood Shop a long term resident of over fifty years opens on Fridays and Saturday's. During the rest of the week you can almost count the shops which are open on the fingers of one hand but on Sunday morning the whole area erupts into life.

In the last few years the Flower Market has broken out of the boundary of Columbia Road and now sprawls around Ezra Street and into every nook, cranny and yard way which can accommodate a shop or a stall.

In 1990 though the market was threatened with closure, like many things in life the market was almost a victim of its own success. At that point in time there were no parking regulations in Tower Hamlets and the marketeers with their huge trucks arrived earlier and earlier and unloaded their stock with little thought for the residents. Their lorries were left running and smoke and fumes belched into our houses. Some of the traders thought nothing of shouting at the top of their voices to each other from five in the morning. Something had to be done. Nobody really wanted closure but the imposition and the mayhem caused by the

above and opposite: *Interior Elwin Street*

parking was intolerable. As many of us commented at the time if there were a fire or the need for an ambulance it would never have been able to get into the area.

Finally strict parking regulations were imposed and market inspectors empowered to ensure that the market did not begin trading much before its official eight thirty start time and end sharply at two. By and large this system works. In the bedding season (May-June) there is a tendency for more trucks to arrive earlier and unload their goods when they shouldn't but at the time of writing we, the residents, are in general at peace with the traders.

The market deserves a book in its own right. The traders come from families who have been using the market for generations. From the early thirties when you secured your Sunday pitch on the blow of a whistle nowadays everything is controlled down to the smallest detail. Who, what and where you pitch is almost set in tablets of stone. It has to be, no longer does the market serve the local populace but the whole of London. It is one of the greatest tourist attractions which the Capital boasts and the range of people who visit it is truly astounding.

By four o'clock in the afternoon though it is all over. Columbia Road is swept clean and washed down. A stray piece of foliage here and there is the only indication that anything has happened.

THE PUBS AND RESTAURANTS SEE THE LAST OF THE VISITORS LEAVE, THE FINAL DUST CART DISAPPEARS AND THE WORLD OF CARS, TECHNOLOGY AND SPEED SUDDENLY SEEMS UNREAL AS THE STREETS SETTLE BACK INTO THEIR OWN TIME WARP. BUILT FROM THE CLAY ON WHICH THEY STAND AND WITNESS TO SO MUCH OVER SO MANY YEARS, UNIQUE THEN, UNIQUE NOW AND SEEMINGLY TIMELESS. LIKE GRAND OLD DAMES SURVEYING THEIR MANSE THEY HAVE SEEN IT ALL, PREJUDICE, LOVE, HATE, WAR AND COMMUNITY; LONG MAY THEY STAND.

Interior Durant Street

ACKNOWLEDGMENTS

We would like to thank all of those people who willingly gave of their time to be interviewed and whose words and photographs form the substance of this book.

We would also like to thank Mike Guida and Stephanie Clarke for helping with the interviews and the Second University trust whose donation helped us to bring this work to completion and finally the wonderful staff at Bancroft Road Local History Library for their patience and help.

REFERENCES:

[1] Inner London Archaeological Unit, Archaeological Survey of Tower Hamlets: Gazette, May 1975 (THLL File 570)

[2] Archaeological Survey of Tower Hamlets; Black, unpag

[3] P. N. Mdx (EPNS), 83 Ekwall Eng. Place names 1960, 40, 212

[4] Guildhall MS 25516, ff 38-39; PRO., E40/7317 ibid. C146/799

[5] AJ Robinson and HB Chesshyre, The Green (1986), 31-5

[6] GLRO., M93/132, f. 1; below, the Green

[7] PRO., E214/602; Hist. MSS. Com .9 Salisbury XV111

[8] MJ Power, Urban development of E. London. 1550-1700 (Lond Univ PhD thesis 1971) 176-9

[9] The diaries of Samuel Pepys ed R. Latham and W Matthews (1980-3) Volume V p 120

[10] ibid Volume VII entries for Sept 1666

Chapter 3 The Estate 1679-1863

Source material about Jesus Hospital Charity The Story of Jesus Hospital Charity in Chipping Barnet 1672-1993. Laurie Adams

[11] The Victorian History of the County of Middlesex Vol XI Early Stepney with Bethnal Green ISBN 019 722910

[12] Cass Library of Victorian Times 8: Sanitary Ramblings by Hector Gavin 1848

Chapter 4 1860-1900

[13] Ragged London in 1861 pub. Smith Elder & Co

[14] Homes in the east of London: A fresh visit to Bethnal-Green; The Builder Jan 28 1871

Chapter 6 The Second World War; Source book for the bombing: Bethnal Green's Ordeal 1939 -1945 by George F Vale 1945: Council of the Metropolitan Borough of Bethnal Green.